TECHNICAL DIFFICULTIES

TECHNICAL DIFFICULTIES

African-American
Notes
on the State of
the Union

JUNE JORDAN

PANTHEON BOOKS
NEW YORK

All rights reserved under International and Pan-American Copyright Conventions. Published in the United States by Pantheon Books, a division of Random House, Inc., New York, and simultaneously in Canada by Random House of Canada Limited, Toronto.

Some essays were previously published as follows: · "For My American Family," originally published in *Newsday*, July 4, 1986. · "Don't Talk About My Momma!" originally published in *Essence*, December 1987. · "Park Slope: Mixing It Up for Good," originally published in *The New York Times*, November 20, 1988. · "America in Confrontation with Democracy, or, The Meaning of the Jesse Jackson Campaign," originally published in the *Village Voice*, November 1988. · "Finding the Way Home" (February 1989), "Wrong or White" (February 1990), "Unrecorded Agonies" (December 1989), "No Chocolates for Breakfast" (April 1989), "Waiting for a Taxi" (June 1989), "The Dance of Revolution" (August 1989), "Where Is the Rage?" (October 1989), "On War and War and . . ." (February 1991), "Can I Get a Witness?" (December 1991), "Toward a New Manifest Destiny" (February 1992), and "Requiem for the Champ" (February 1992), originally published in *The Progressive*, Madison, Wisconsin.

Acknowledgments of permission to quote previously published material are on page 227.

Library of Congress Cataloging–in–Publication Data
Jordan, June, 1936–
    Technical difficulties : African-American notes on the state of
the union / June Jordan.
    p. cm.   1 6 0 2 2 3 2 9 8 1
    ISBN 0-679-40625-5
    1. United States—Civilization—1970– 2. United States—Politics
and government—1981–1989. 3. Afro-Americans—Politics and
government. I. Title.
E169.12.J657 1991
973.92—dc20   91-52656

Book design by Jan Melchior
Manufactured in the United States of America
First Edition

DEDICATED
WITH MY LOVE
TO CHRISTOPHER
AND
TO ADRIENNE

CONTENTS

CONTENTS

ACKNOWLEDGMENTS

To Matthew Rothschild,
my friend and publisher of *The Progressive*,
and to Margaret Wan-ling Lin,
my friend and political comrade

TECHNICAL DIFFICULTIES

For My American Family

A Belated Tribute
to a Legacy
of Gifted Intelligence
and Guts

I WOULD LOVE TO SEE PICTURES OF THE STATUE OF LIBERTY taken by my father. They would tell me so much about him that I wish I knew. He couldn't very well ask that lady to "hold that smile" or "put on a little something with red to brighten it up." He'd have to take her "as is," using a choice of angles or focus or distance as the means to his statement. And I imagine that my father would choose a long-shot, soft-focus, wide-angle lens: that would place Miss Liberty in her full formal setting, and yet suggest the tears that easily spilled from his eyes whenever he spoke about "this great country of ours: America."

This essay, written April 29, 1986, was originally published in a special section of *New York Newsday,* July 4, 1986.

A camera buff, not averse to wandering around the city with both a Rolleiflex and a Rolleicord at the ready, my father thought nothing of a two or three hours' "setup" for a couple of shots of anything he found beautiful. I remember one Saturday, late morning, when I watched my father push the "best" table in the house under the dining-room windows, fidget the venetian blinds in order to gain the most interesting, slatted light, and then bring the antique Chinese vase downstairs from the parlor, fill that with fresh roses from the backyard, and then run out to the corner store for several pieces of fruit to complete his still-life composition.

All of this took place in the 1940s. We lived in the Bedford-Stuyvesant neighborhood of Brooklyn, one of the largest urban Black communities in the world. Besides the fruit and the flowers of my father's aesthetic preoccupation, and just beyond those narrow brownstone dining-room windows, there was a burly mix of unpredictable street life that he could not control, despite incessant telephone calls, for example, to the Department of Sanitation: "Hello. This is a man by the name of Granville Ivanhoe Jordan, and I'm calling about garbage collection. What happened? Did you forget?!"

The unlikely elements of my father's name may summarize his history and character rather well. Jordan is a fairly common surname on the island of Jamaica where he was born, one of perhaps twelve or thirteen children who foraged for food, and who never forgot, or forgave, the ridicule his ragged clothing provoked in school. Leaving the classroom long before the normal conclusion to an elementary education, my father later taught himself to read and, after that, he never stopped reading and reading everything he could find, from Burpee seed catalogues to Shakespeare to the *National Geographic* magazines to "Negro" poetry to liner notes for the record albums of classical music that he devoured. But he was also "the little bull"—someone who loved a good rough fight and who even volunteered to teach boxing to other young "Negroes" at the Harlem YMCA, where he frequently participated in political and militant "uplifting-the-race" meetings, on West 135th Street.

Except for weekends, my father pursued all of his studies in the long early hours of the night, 3 or 4 A.M., after eight hours' standing up at the post office where he speed-sorted mail quite without the assistance of computers and zip codes which, of course, had yet to be invented. Exceptionally handsome and exceptionally vain, Mr. G. I. Jordan, immaculate in one of his innumerable, rooster-elegant suits, would readily hack open a coconut with a machete, or slice a grapefruit in half, throw his head back, and squeeze the juice into his mouth—carefully held a tricky foot away—all to my mother's head-shaking dismay: "Why now you have to act up like a monkey chaser, eh?"

It is a sad thing to consider that this country has given its least to those who have loved it the most. I am the daughter of West Indian immigrants. And perhaps there are other Americans as believing and as grateful and as loyal, but I doubt it. In general, the very word *immigrant* connotes somebody white, while *alien* denotes everybody else. But hundreds and hundreds of thousands of Americans are hardworking, naturalized Black citizens whose trust in the democratic promise of the mainland has never been reckoned with, fully, or truly reciprocated. For instance, I know that my parents would have wanted to say, "Thanks, America!" if only there had been some way, some public recognition and welcome of their presence, here, and then some really big shot to whom their gratitude might matter.

I have seen family snapshots of my mother pushing me in a baby carriage decorated with the single decal F.D.R., and I have listened to endless tall stories about what I did or didn't do when my father placed me in the lap of New York's mayor,

Fiorello La Guardia, and, on top of the ornate wallpaper of our parlor floor there was a large color photograph of the archbishop of the Episcopal diocese of Long Island; my parents lived in America, full of faith.

When I visited the birthplace of my mother, twelve years ago, I was embarrassed by the shiny rented car that brought me there: even in 1974, there were no paved roads in Clonmel, a delicate dot of a mountain village in Jamaica. And despite the breathtaking altitude, you could not poke or peer yourself into a decent position for "a view": the vegetation was that dense, that lush, and that chaotic. On or close to the site of my mother's childhood home, I found a neat wood cabin, still without windowpanes or screens, a dirt floor, and a barefoot family of seven, quietly bustling about.

I was stunned. There was neither electricity nor running water. How did my parents even hear about America, more than a half century ago? In the middle of the Roaring Twenties, these eager Black immigrants came, by boat. Did they have to borrow shoes for the journey?

I know that my aunt and my mother buckled into domestic work, once they arrived, barely into their teens. I'm not sure how my father managed to feed himself before that fantastic 1933 afternoon when he simply ran all the way from midtown Manhattan up to our Harlem apartment, shouting out the news: A job! He had found a job!

And throughout my childhood I cannot recall even one utterance of disappointment, or bitterness with America. In fact, my parents hid away any newspaper or magazine article that dealt with "jim crow" or "lynchings" or "discrimination." These were terms of taboo status neither to be spoken nor explained to me. Instead I was given a child's biography of Abraham Lincoln and the Bible stories of Daniel and David, and, from my father, I learned about Marcus Garvey and George Washington Carver and Mary McLeod Bethune. The focus was relentlessly upbeat. Or, as Jimmy Cliff used to sing it, "You can make it if you really try."

My mother's emphasis was more religious, and more consistently race-conscious, and she was equally affirmative: God would take care of me. And, besides, there was ("C'mon, Joe! C'mon!") the Brown Bomber, Joe Louis, and then, incredibly, Jackie Robinson who, by himself, elevated the Brooklyn Dodgers into a sacred cult worshipped by apparently dauntless Black baseball fans.

We had a pretty rich life. Towards the end of the 1960s I was often amazed by facile references to Black communities as "breeding grounds of despair" or "culturally deprived" or "ghettos." That was not the truth. There are grounds for despair in the suburbs, evidently, and I more than suspect greater cultural deprivation in economically and racially and socially homogeneous Long Island commuter towns than anything I ever had to overcome!

In Bedford-Stuyvesant, I learned all about white history and white literature, but I lived and learned about my own, as well. My father marched me to the American Museum of Natural History and to the Planetarium, at least twice a month, while my mother picked up "the slack" by riding me, by trolley car, to public libraries progressively farther and farther away from our house. In the meantime, on our own block of Hancock Street, between Reid and Patchen avenues, we had rice and peas and curried lamb or, upstairs, in my aunt and uncle's apartment, pigs' feet and greens. On the piano in the parlor there was boogie-woogie, blues, and Chopin. Across the street, there were cold-water flats that included the Gumbs family or, more precisely, Donnie Gumbs, whom I saw as the inarguable paragon of masculine cute. There were "American Negroes," and "West Indians." Some rented their housing, and some were buying their homes. There were Baptists, Holy Rollers, and Episcopalians, side by side.

On that same one block, Father Coleman, the minister of our church, lived and worked as the first Black man on New York's Board of Higher Education. There was Mrs. Taylor, whose music studio was actually a torture chamber into which many of us were forced for piano lessons. And a Black policeman. And a mail carrier. And a doctor. And my beloved Uncle Teddy, with a Doctor of Law degree from Fordham University. And the tiny, exquisite arrow of my aunt, who became one of the first Black principals in the entire New York City public school system. And my mother, who had been president of the first Black class to graduate from the Lincoln School of Nursing, and my father, who earned the traditional gold watch as a retiring civil servant, and Nat King Cole and calypso and boyfriends and Sunday School and confirmation and choir and stickball and roller skates and handmade wooden scooters and marbles and make-believe tea parties and I cannot recall feeling underprivileged, or bored, in that "ghetto."

And from such "breeding grounds of despair," Negro men volunteered, in droves, for active duty in an army that did not want or honor them. And from such "limited" communities, Negro women, such as my mother, left their homes in every kind of weather, and at any hour, to tend to the ailing and heal the sick, regardless of their color, or ethnicity. And in such a "culturally deprived" house as that modest home created by my parents, I became an American poet.

And in the name of my mother and my father, I want to say thanks to America. And I want something more:

My aunt has survived the deaths of her husband and my parents in typical, if I may say so, West Indian fashion. Now in her seventies, and no longer principal of a New York City public school, she rises at 5 A.M., every morning, to prepare for another day of complicated duties as the volunteer principal of a small Black private academy. In the front yard of her home in the Crown Heights section of Brooklyn, the tulips and buttercups have begun to bloom already. Soon every passerby will see her azaleas and jonquils and irises blossoming under the Japanese maple tree and around the base of the Colorado blue spruce.

She is in her seventies, and she tells me:

I love the United States and I always will uphold it as a place of opportunity. This is not to say that you won't meet prejudice along the way but it's up to you to overcome it. And it can be overcome!

Well, I think back to Clonmel, Jamaica, and I visualize my aunt skipping along the goat tracks, fast as she can, before the darkness under the banana tree leaves becomes too scary for a nine-year-old. Or I think about her, struggling to fetch water from the river, in a pail. And I jump-cut to Orange High School, New Jersey, U.S.A., where my aunt maintained a 95 average, despite her extracurricular activities as a domestic, and where she was denied the valedictory because, as the English teacher declared, "You have an accent that the parents will not understand." And I stay quiet as my aunt explains, "I could have let that bother me, but I said, 'Naw, I'm not gone let this keep me down!' "

And what I want is to uphold this America, this beckoning and this shelter provided by my parents and my aunt. I want to say thank you to them, my faithful American family.

Waking Up in the Middle of Some American Dreams

I have rejected propaganda teaching me about the beautiful
the truly rare:

Supposedly the ocean at the hushpoint of the shore
supposedly
the ocean at the hushpoint of the shore
is beautiful
for instance
but the beautiful can stay out there
unless I see
a bird seize sandflies
or your self
approach me
laughing out a sound to spoil
the pretty picture . . .

—June Jordan, from "Poem on a New Year's Eve"

This was the keynote address at the Agenda for the 90s Conference in Portland, Oregon, May 18, 1986.

I REMEMBER LIVING IN A COASTAL WILDERNESS, BY MYSELF. No one could see the little house from the road. And all that I could see, looking through the long glass walls that frequently confused the birds, was wildlife sanctuary marsh, bay waters, and an always restless, unpredictable sky. Occasionally, a hawk would shudder and soar, his huge wings inches from my face. More often, one or another jackrabbit would try to adopt me, daily hopping closer and closer to my car until I had to teach it to beware of creatures like myself.

Day and night I pursued my lonely "constitutionals": those mile-and-a-half to two-mile compulsive treks leading to a completely uninhabited beach laden with crunchy shell-life, under foot. By December or January, these unremarkable habits thrust me into bitter, howling circumstances such that I easily imagined my body an eroded, baffling skeleton flung next to the carcass, say, of a horseshoe crab. But whether it was December or April or July, whenever the moon failed to appear, that unmitigated, that waiting darkness outside aroused every one of my instincts for panic, and flight. And yet, I did not run. Nor did I abandon any of my rather demanding outdoor routines. I think I was practicing to cross the Rocky Mountains. Or I think I was trying to learn something intimate about the Long March of the Chinese revolutionaries. Or I think I was, rather obliquely, to be sure, training myself for a different, a social kind of duress. Or I think I was immersing myself in privacy paradise, East Coast.

I did not have a dog. Or a cat. I almost had no phone, as I hardly ever bothered to answer it and not too many people bothered to call. Regularly I would finish a poem and then drive from my house, at two or three o'clock in the morning, to the post office in town. That was my notion of a pretty exciting Friday or Saturday night, in fact. And I also remember another artist, an American painter whose name has risen now, as illustrious as that of Pablo Picasso's. I remember that elder kinsman who also lived in that wilderness and who, more or less once a month, would drink a whole bottle of booze, mount his three-speed bicycle, and then attempt to ride it, straight down the white line dividing the main highway. I thought he was just a wee bit crazy; as for me, I thought I was lucky. I knew about him after all: somebody older and wiser who lived by himself, somebody who had surrounded himself with acres and acres of private property on which he could keep an enormous, silent house. As for me, I could walk to the beach in any season of the year and find nobody else, ever, on the sand. If I sat quite still in the evenings, I could hear the spiders weaving their webs. And I thought I was lucky.

One day a feature writer for a Long Island newspaper came to interview and photograph me "at home." My first doubts about my paradise of privacy arose when I saw the published story, complete with a photograph depicting me absolutely alone among a million tall marsh reeds. I looked and I looked at that strange picture: Was that really the idea? Was that really the world of my dreams? To my credit, however dim, I did suspect a lunatic skew to that photograph, that summary of my place, my role. Nevertheless, truly traditional/deranged/ American images of the good life kept me in that wilderness, that willful loneliness, until somebody else came into the little house and raped me. I remember thinking that there was no point to a scream, there was no point to struggling towards those enormous clear windows. There was nobody, anywhere around, to help. And afterwards, when I could make myself talk again, I crawled to the telephone and placed two long-distance calls: there was nobody local who would care.

That brilliant elder artist applied himself to a huge canvas taunting his vision and his craft, seven days a week. In fact, he never took a day off, or a vacation. And, of course, I respected him, completely. Once, when I asked him why he worked that way, without respite, he shrugged his shoulders, "What else is there to do?" I remember absorbing his response as ultimate proof of his wisdom and of his genius as a human being: He lived alone. He worked all of the time. He was famous. He was rich. Nobody disturbed him. Nobody lived close enough to try. By our American standards he had become indisputably successful. Soon people in general would refer to him as A Great Man. Already, international critics proclaimed him an exemplar, a positive legend of our century. And I, twenty-five to thirty years his junior, I turned away from the flickering question: What does it mean to be a legend to all and a friend to none?

And I, a young Black woman poet, duly emulated the isolating rigors of his artistic commitment. Didn't everyone approve, if not admire, the ostracizing dedication of his art? Did he not have a child whom he seldom saw? Did I not have a son whom I saw, seldom? What besides race and sex and class could block me from becoming a clearly successful American, A Great White Man? Now, in that wilderness period of my life, no one ever disturbed the expensive isolation of the famous painter. But someone raped me in the middle of my rented, pseudo–Walden Pond. Someone had insinuated himself into that awkward, tiny shelter of my thoughts and dreams. He had dealt with me as egotistically as, in another way, I had postponed dealing with anyone besides myself. He had overpowered the supposed protection of my privacy, he had violated the boundaries of my single self. He had acted as though nothing mattered so much as his certainly brute impulse. And was that conduct entirely different from my own, supposing that nothing mattered as much as my artistic impulse, the one that ruled my friends and my family and my neighbors out of my usual universe?

That famous painter guarded himself against trespass while I tried to protect myself from all violation. But dangers of trespass did not push The Great Man out on a highway, drunk on his bike. Nor was possible violation of my person the underlying threat to my isolated life-style. On the contrary: what jeopardized his and my safety, and our happiness, was the absence of connections between us and the absence of a sharing, a dependency between the two of us and other people who would care about us because we cared about them.

American illusions of autonomy, American delusions of individuality, seduced the painter into monthly bouts of arrogance and potential suicide. These same American illusions held me, finally, a prisoner to the merciless whimsies of a rapist in my home.

Not only did that painter/that father and this poet/this mother believe ourselves eminently respectable in the conscientiously selfish design of our days, we considered ourselves virtuous and self-sacrificing. The very obvious, deep, social deficiencies of our lives merely convinced each of us that we must be profoundly inspired, if not exalted, in our ambitious, unremitting labors.

So it seems to me that I am not entirely different from the painter or the rapist. Misbegotten American dreams have maimed us all. And one of these, especially, continues to distort and paralyze our simplest capabilities for cooperation as a species. Beloved, national myths about you and me as gloriously rugged, independent individuals pervade our consciousness. Every one of us knows that, to whatever extent she is worthy of affection or praise or promotion or functional housing or a faithful husband or respect or diligent medical attention or honest car repair or satisfactory sex or civil civil servants (such as mannerly policemen or courteous desk clerks in the Office of Social Security) or sensitive legal counsel or accurate political representation or a safe and beautiful community or a 100 percent perfect day in the country—perfect weather perfect traffic conditions perfect timing—every one of us knows that, to whatever extent he or she secures any of the above, it happens not because he is a God-given human being, not because she is an American citizen, not because he has worked hard at a dumb job for fifteen years and never knowingly hurt or cheated anybody, not because she has done her best, always, to be good: a good girl, a good friend, a good date, a good lover a good wife a good mother: Every American one of us knows that these fundamental and democratic amenities of existence will fall into your lap because, as our most popular greeting cards express it, again and again: You're different. I'm different. You're special. I'm special. Every single American grows up believing that, in the happy ending ahead of us, we will just gleefully dust our classmates and our fellow workers and our compatriots and then, to really mix up the metaphors, we will leave them grounded, like so many ugly ducklings, while we wheel and speed and plummet and, steadily glittering, rise: 235 million Jonathan Livingston Seagulls with nary a thought for the welfare of the flock, or companionship, or a resting or a nesting environment!

The flipside of this delusional disease, this infantile and apparently implacable trust in mass individuality, is equally absurd, and destructive. Because every American one of us is different and special, it follows that every problem or crisis is exclusively our own, or, conversely, your problem—not mine.

Anywhere U.S.A. and you may, easily, imagine a gigantic traffic jam: somebody's radiator overheats and he turns off the engine, thereby blocking several cars directly behind him. One of the other drivers approaches the disabled vehicle. "What's the matter?" he asks. The man inside the car points to the smoke escaping from under the hood. "You can see for yourself," he says. The other driver snaps back, "That's your problem! Get it out of my way!" Or, look at the Civil Rights Movement. I personally know of hundreds of Negro mothers and fathers who failed forever, as it seemed to us, their children, before they would admit:

a. That they survived desperate barriers to their pursuit of happiness.

b. That these barriers issued from racist loathing of us, regardless whether we practiced the piano or shined our shoes.

As though the horror and the dread of lynching and jim crow translated into something shameful about the victims, something the victims must keep secret, terrible years passed before these parents, mine among them, realized that they must publicly proclaim and publicly protest all of the injustice that their worn hands, slumped shoulders, and lowered eyes made clear. And even more time passed before these victims recognized the need to act, collectively, against that outside evil force of hatred.

The Women's Movement has suffered from comparably personal assumptions: I am inherently special and different from every other woman in my neighborhood. No one else feels stranded in her own living room. No one else has been raped by a friend. No other woman's husband beats her up. I am the only woman blithely threatened by her boss with sexual propositions or demands. I am the only female no one listens to. And so I do not speak about my terror or my boredom. I do not acknowledge the common nature of my female predicament. I do not join with other women to deliver myself from the consequences of sexist contempt and nationwide institutions of misogyny. And so it goes, as well, for each elderly American who can no longer take care of himself, and each family with teenagers addicted to drugs, and each household of the suddenly unemployed, and each person married to an alcoholic.

Do we not live in the generous, pastoral land of the Marlboro Man? The land of healthy and good-looking and young people who ski and sail and laugh and smoke cigarettes, all at the same time, gracefully? If we do not match up to those images, then we have personally failed, somehow. And, naturally, you keep personal failure a secret.

American delusions of individuality now disfigure our national landscape with multitudes of disconnected pained human beings who pull down the shades on prolonged and needless agony. But if we would speak the unspeakable, if we would name and say the source of our sorrow and scars, we would find a tender and a powerful company of others struggling as we do, and we would know we should show to the world, at last, that shame belongs with blame, not on the victim.

We would undertake collective political action founded on admitted similarities and grateful connections among us, otherwise needful citizens who now regard each other as burdensome or frightening or irrelevant. This would mean a great national coming out—a coming out of our cars, a coming out of our deadpan passage through the streets of America, a coming out of the suburbs, a coming out of our perverted enthusiasm for whatever keeps us apart: home computers, answering machines, VCRs, and then the proverbial two weeks in a faraway cabin in the woods.

But each American one of us feels so special and so different that none of us assumes the validity of his or her outrage or longing inside the mythical context of "the American Mainstream." We become persuaded that the people of our country must be somebody else, not you and me, even as we regard our government as some alien, half-deaf, and unaccountable monarch to whom we—sooner or later—must pay homage or, at least, taxes. We tolerate insulting, homicidal proposals for national security—such as an aircraft carrier or a helmet and a bulletproof vest—when what we know is that national security must mean, for example, respectful and adequate and guaranteed tender care for elderly Americans and for any American one of us who cannot, by herself, do things without help. And meanwhile our American worship of space, open road space, frontier space, astral space and, more particularly, as much space as possible between me and whoever you are— on the bus, on my block, on my job, in my field—our American dreams of "the first" and "the only" produce an invariably mistaken self-centered perspective that repeatedly proves to be self-defeating and, even, antidemocratic. *Demos,* as in democratic, as in a democratic state, means people, not person. A democratic nation of persons, of individuals, is an impossibility, and a fratricidal goal. Each American one of us must consciously choose to become a willing and outspoken part of *the people* who, together, will determine our individual chances for happiness, and justice.

By *people* I mean the white people the Black people the female people the lonely people the terrorized people the elderly people the young people the visionary people the unemployed people the regular ordinary omnipresent people who crave grace and variety and surprise and safety and one new day after another.

Democratic anything presupposes equal membership in the body politic. But we will never even approximate the equality a democratic state depends upon, we will never even understand the equality each American one of us requires for our rightful self-respect, as long as we will deny all that we feel and need in common.

But I'm special. I'm different, just like you. I worried about putting together these sentences I have written, here, from my heart: What was the point? To whom should I present myself? What can I know of the doubts and the aching and the bitterness that may prey upon a middle-class nuclear family living in, for instance, Portland, Oregon?

And then I understood that the question was, rather, do I care? And then I understood that the answer is yes, yes, yes: I care because I want you to care about me. I care because I have become aware of my absolute dependency upon you, whoever you are, for the quality and the outcome of my social, my democratic experience.

And even if the white or Black nuclear families of Portland wanted to reject my offering as oddball ruminations beyond the perimeters of relevant American national fact, I know, rationally, that I am as ordinary as the rest of that majority of American women who are full-time employed, I know that I am as normal as the other seventeen million Americans of the fastest-growing segment of our total population who compose single-parent and single-adult households and I know that the United States already needs some twenty million new housing units to accommodate our single status, because we will not disappear. And whether elderly or middle-aged or young, most of us can neither afford the money nor the labor-intensive upkeep nor the costly isolation that currently dominant modes of American dreaming imply. But still I am worried: I am so special and I am so different, just like you. I am different from the American dreams of individuality and space that have tortured my strivings. I am special, apparently, because the sum of my considerable, so-called individual success means that I have just received a letter from my lover whom I have not seen in three weeks, I have just written a letter to my son whom I will not see until a month from now, my friends send me photographs so that I will not forget them, I cannot afford the long-distance phone calls I must make whenever I need anything urgent, my kitchen table is strewn with plane tickets and airport-to-airport itineraries, and I have scheduled an appointment to visit my aunt sometime during the summer. Even as I compose this essay, this offering to strangers on whom I must rely for the sake of my usefulness and living connection, what I can hear, most clearly, is the ticking of the kitchen clock, and the inanimate whirring of the refrigerator: I am living by myself, in America.

I am a Black woman poet who has organized her American life not unlike the life of any successful, white orthopedic surgeon whose secretary will leave you feeling embarrassed if you ask to speak with him, directly, or if you suggest that eight weeks is too long to wait for a fifteen-minute consultation. I am a Black woman poet living in an American-dream white cottage with tulips and hyacinth and violets blooming yellow and red and purple and lovely next to the front door and, . . . inside that ideal, spotless, American house there is no one besides me and my answering machine and my VCR. I do not even get to say hello to the wife of my landlord who lives in the big house, the only other house on this ideal American estate of eight-and-a-half acres. The landlord's wife drives her Cherokee Chief down to the mailbox, next to the stone gate with the elegantly lettered sign that reads PRIVATE: NO ADMITTANCE [*sic*], and then backs the jeep up the lengthy driveway, alone and oblivious, past the cottage where I sit watching her as I watch the squirrels, the doves, and the crows who dart about, also singly and oblivious.

I had thought that the city was inhospitable to average yearnings for a happy life. But I have learned, firsthand, about the wilderness of the suburbs. I had thought I wanted, and perhaps deserved, to live in a house. But I have learned that a house is not a community.

When I was still a young woman, I asked my friend and mentor, R. Buckminster Fuller, about the several wristwatches that he always wore, simultaneously. He described to me his incessant, global peregrinations and explained his wish to ascertain, easily, what time it might be anywhere on the planet. I listened to him, puzzled, and without envy. But why, I wondered, would anybody travel like that; didn't he have a home? Didn't home matter to him? "A man is not a tree," he told me. And in the decades since that conversation I have gradually, and the hard way, comprehended what he meant: The whole world will become a home to all of us, or none of us can hope to live on it, peacefully. But much of the American dream mistakenly supposes that, like a tree, we will grow and flourish, standing in one place where we murmur doomed declarations about our roots, about finding our roots, or putting down roots. In fact, of course, if we remain where we start from we will neither grow nor flourish. And much of the American dream furthermore supposes that our children are, as we like to say, seeds. But, again, that is a peculiar metaphor for human beings who must change and challenge the old order of things into which we are born or we must forfeit our value as new and innocent life in the world.

And if we will claim the whole world as our living room, then it seems to me that we must alter our strangely American concepts of family and home, and we must make these alterations quickly!

This is the moment when we might intelligently exhume earlier systems of extended kinship and then stretch those systems into something suitable for the twenty-first century. Beginning with the given—the physically familiar and comfortable family that we discover as our own—we will have to cultivate courage enough to reach for and then to embrace the unexpected, the uncontrollable, the completely unfamiliar kinsmen and women who must either become our comrades or our enemies, as we work to preserve the species. Television satellites, nuclear missiles, and grievously felt contrasts between a two-car garage and famine will not permit us to do less. And so I submit to you that, in a democratic state, the city is not a mistake: our cities are not optional elements of a democratic civilization! We cannot leave behind us our failures to gratify our individual needs in the context of a heterogeneous, millionfold population. That is, exactly, the task of a rational democracy. That is, precisely, the task of any American one of us hoping to grow and flourish among equals with whom we can make, and keep, life-saving connections. We must learn how to satisfy our individual needs in the context of a heterogeneous, equally entitled, millionfold population of our peers. I am waking up in the middle of some American dreams that have tormented most of us throughout most of our American history!

Several times while writing this paper, my phone has rung and I have sprung forward to pick up the receiver. I am vacating the premises of this idyllic cottage. I am moving back to the city and I hope that one of the incoming calls will let me hear good news: news of an apartment smack in the middle of an unruly mix of other Americans who manage, somehow, *not* to act on brute impulse and not to expect others to submit to our stupefying images of ourselves as more special and more different than anyone else.

I look forward to my return to this new American dream, this dream of the civilized metropolis that will validate the democratic state. There I will have less time for theory (and which American one of us is somebody theoretical?) and there I will have more and more direct contact, direct conflict, to which I will have to react, remembering that the only escape from such difficult groundwork is fantasy. There I may become less "successful" but there I may hope to recover more of the actual touch of tenderness. There, in our American city, I am less likely to stare, like a retarded barbarian, at somebody who is an Arab or someone who is Filipino, or someone who speaks Spanish. As I awaken from my misbegotten dreams, I am planning to stop my American habits of genteel make-believe: I will not pretend that I do not understand terror, or terrorism. I will not pretend that it is privacy and fame and quiet that I want when what I need is a sanitary, a safe and reliable subway or public bus system, an attractive apartment that I can afford to rent, a clean and welcoming community Laundromat, a local and an inexpensive, crowded restaurant, and other different hundreds and thousands of unknown but knowable Americans always around me. And then, as often as possible, at night, I want and I need an ostensible stranger who will lie beside me becoming someone I love at least as much as I love myself.

I do not believe that these new American dreams of mine mark me as special, or different. In these longings, and in this faith, I do not believe that I am living alone in America. But you will have to let me know: Am I?

OF THOSE

SO CLOSE BESIDE ME,

WHICH ARE YOU?

I wake to sleep, and take my waking slow.
I feel my fate in what I cannot fear.
I learn by going where I have to go.

We think by feeling. What is there to know?
I hear my being dance from ear to ear.
I wake to sleep, and take my waking slow.

Of those so close beside me, which are you?
God bless the Ground! I shall walk softly there,
And learn by going where I have to go.

Light takes the Tree; but who can tell us how?
The lowly worm climbs up a winding stair;
I wake to sleep, and take my waking slow.

Great Nature has another thing to do
To you and me, so take the lively air,
And, lovely, learn by going where to go.

This shaking keeps me steady. I should know.
What falls away is always. And is near.
I wake to sleep, and take my waking slow.
I learn by going where I have to go.

—Theodore Roethke, "The Waking"

This was the commencement address at the University of California, Berkeley, on May 17, 1986.

EVEN ON THIS BEAUTIFUL AFTERNOON IN BEAUTIFUL, SUNLIT Berkeley, some of you may wonder, "What does beauty mean to this world?" Can it hurt, or help, anyone? Will a sense of beauty ever save, or threaten, my life? As Roethke asks, "Of those so close beside me, which are you? / God bless the Ground! I shall walk softly there . . ."

As an undergraduate I don't think any such straightforward question ever troubled my ecstatic, disorderly notions about the nature of my studies. I crammed Doric columns and tonic chords and definitions of a sonnet or a sestina into my head because I had to, and because I rather liked the way that information settled inside my otherwise drafty skull. It felt good. And I suppose that I believed I would become a better, or more of a good, person in direct relation to how much I learned about the measurable means to somebody's idea of beauty. I never harbored any inclination to discredit these ideas. Certainly they were not my own, but mine were scarcely under development. I did not doubt but that, once a lovely evidence for new ideas arrived, those anonymous caretakers of Western culture would welcome them and place them eagerly alongside the old. That so many people so loved a poem or a temple or a sonata that they would bother themselves until they had fathomed the structure of the work, and then preserve, somehow, in perpetuity, this invented thing that they found beautiful, seemed to me natural, inherently harmless, and reassuring. I was, after all, a young artist—a young writer—myself!

I even encountered Sir Gawain and all the Ladies and Love Lost and Paradise Lost and something called heroic couplets with a modest excitement somewhat beyond equanimity. I found English literature peculiar and quite interesting in the same way that I found dugout canoes, and cooking utensils, and tepees of Native Americans peculiar and quite interesting when I first saw those artifacts. And while you can't drink water out of a sonnet, and while strict iambic pentameter has never struck me as plainly more important than the craft requirements for an accurate bow and arrow, I always assumed that, one day, we would also share, and learn how to cherish, the chants and the songs and the stories of Native Americans: I did not suppose inherent conflict between those implements for survival and the cultural tools that document, interpret, and importantly adorn—or beautify—a people's wish to survive.

As an undergraduate English major I did notice certain exclusions from the literature; mores and passions of the English, the Irish, the prerevolutionary Russian, and the French seemed to monopolize our weekly and regular assignments. On the other hand, American, German, Japanese, Scandinavian, and African writers appeared, if at all, on our optional reading lists. Since I certainly felt closer to Steinbeck's Okies than I did to Dostoevsky's Grushenka, I never concluded anything about the standard curriculum readings except that the English faculty tended to teach whatever the faculty had studied a long, limited time ago. It never occurred to me that optional reading lists might actually imply that somebody powerful really believed there were optional people alive on the planet.

I guess I was very young, when I was an English major.

Only a few years after college, I attended a fairly hotshot cocktail party at which American poets such as John Ciardi and Robert Penn Warren and William Meredith absolutely amazed me by the quantity of bourbon they could, evidently, consume without losing consciousness, or mannerly deportment. Chitchat among these great men gravitated towards the pros or cons of wearing pajamas. I distinctly remember one of the more illustrious poets asserting that he was, in fact, "a pajama man." The drinking continued, along with much, let's call it worldly, merrymaking until a tall Black man that someone identified as Ralph Ellison caused the entire room to quiet down, completely. He was angry. He spoke with clipped, deliberate syllables; "All of this means nothing! Look at Germany! All of that music, all of that poetry, and those novels and the paintings and did any of it ever stop a single Nazi from pushing a single human being into the oven?" Nobody said a word. I could hardly breathe. Wasn't there anyone in that Pantheon gathering who could answer him?

I think it was Bill Meredith who finally ventured a response: "But why are you writing, if that's what you feel—"

Ellison interrupted with "I don't know!" He was practically livid. "Show me the poem," he persisted, "tell me the name of the opera/the symphony that will stop one man from killing another man and then maybe"—he gestured towards the elegant, bejeweled assembly with his hand that held a cut-crystal glass of scotch—"just maybe some of this can be justified!"

As I remember that New York evening, twenty-five years ago, Ellison's explosion met with considerable indignation: Did he seriously want to suggest that artists need to justify their art? And so forth. But I didn't listen to the rest of it; Ellison had shocked me to the bone. I felt pretty small and pretty stupid. I stood near those penthouse windows overlooking the city and for the first time I felt the agony of the absurd: I could not count upon a goodness inherent to anything I knew or anything I hoped to do. And I plunged myself into imaginings of Nazi Germany, and I riveted my hunted hated body right there, in World War II, and I conjured up the blackouts and the warning sirens and the horror of the pounding on the doors and there I remained trapped and searching among the years and years of reading and memorization of our literature for something that would help me not to surrender.

And something did come back to me—from *Hamlet:*

The bird of dawning singeth all night long;
And then, they say, no spirit can walk abroad,

The nights are wholesome; then no planets strike,
No fairy takes, nor witch hath power to charm,
So hallow'd and so gracious is the time.[1]

And I'm sorry I was much too shy to offer that to Mr. Ellison. He has written very little, indeed, after that evening, and after his own *Invisible Man*. I wish I could have told him what I now understand: that we do not sweat and summon our best in order to rescue the killers; it is to comfort and to empower the possible victims of evil that we do tinker and daydream and revise and memorize and then impart all that we can of our inspired, our inherited, humanity.

Because it is now a quarter of a century later and I still do not recognize a necessary conflict between the sonnet and the bow and arrow. I do not accept that immersion into our collective quest for things beautiful will cripple our own abilities to honor the right of all human beings to survive.

But as I look at you young American graduates today, I wonder what you will decide about our heritage. How is it possible that, again and again, the university that requires you to humbly examine and analyze and savor and assimilate the tiniest facts about Anna Karenina—a woman who never even caught a cold, as a matter of fact—because she was never real life, as you are, as I am, how it is possible that the same university should express its astonishment and brutal chagrin whenever you have elected to turn away from Tolstoi's make-believe and commit your most intelligent attention, for one promising moment, to the real life and the real death of human beings in Concord, in Seattle, in Des Moines, in Detroit, in Juigalpa, in Soweto?

Student friends of mine, here at the University of California, Berkeley, have kindly forwarded press clippings from the April

[1]*Hamlet,* act 1, scene 1, lines 153–57.

1986 confrontations between student demonstrations against apartheid and university agents of control: the Berkeley police. I have looked and looked at those photographs. I have grieved from my heart for those young moral heroes and heroines depicted there, attempting to escape a nightstick, or fallen from a smashed kneecap, or somersaulted backwards as these agents of control overturned and tore up a pitiful South African shanty facsimile, in front of California Hall. What is the source of their courage? Where do you get your ideas of character, of honor, of a beautiful and a just human life? And shall we omit or forget those poems, those stories that lead a young white man, wearing glasses, to raise his fist, even as he walks into a courtroom for arraignment at the Santa Rita County jail? I look at this new, this—I would say—well-educated, young white American and I hear myself imploring my peers to acknowledge him, properly: *This bird of dawning singeth all night long*—all night long until apartheid shall cease to exist upon the earth! And how should any of us who perpetuate the humanities in any form, how should we be surprised, or why should we be offended, that those whom we have taught to love beauty, to care about Anna Karenina, and Hamlet, and the daffodils, and Paradise Lost, should hate and abhor what is ugly and killing and cowardly? If you do not actively oppose and reject every system and every deed that you must deem inhumane, then I believe you have been poorly educated; we have not taught you well; and you must now teach yourself new poems, new stories, and new craft requirements that will certify your own defensible humanity. Sixteen years and thirteen days ago, a young American student, Allison Krause, silently placed a flower inside the rifle of a state trooper standing on emergency alert, at Kent State University. Within minutes of that act, she was dead. Was that a metaphor? Was she, perhaps, an English major? Did that compelling small gesture of Allison Krause violate the state trooper's ideas of beauty and order? Or did he possess any such ideas? Had he ever heard of metaphors, or similes, or human beings who were never optional in some actual country that their lives required, a country called Cambodia? What was his training in the humanities?

At Kent State, there is a memorial to the four unarmed students murdered by state troopers, May 4, 1970. The memorial amounts to "subtractions from the earth." As the *Kent Stater* reports in its April 8, 1986 issue, "Subtracted from the earth are four circular rooms representative of the absences of Allison Krause, Jeffrey Miller, Sandra Scheuer and William Schroeder. These sanctuaries nestled in the hillside are places for reflection and contemplation: a container, a refuge or home for spirits scattered many years ago in a parking lot."

I am honored to stand before you, today, and to gaze upon your spirits gathered here with so much rightful pride and positive expectation. May you never become "subtractions from the earth." May you always walk the world with hope, and with the humanity of kindness, and with an insatiable desire for justice, everywhere. As the poet Theodore Roethke has written:

Of those so close beside me, which are you?
God bless the Ground! I shall walk softly there . . .

Good luck to you. Good luck to all of us!

WHERE ARE WE

AND WHOSE COUNTRY

IS THIS, ANYWAY?

TWO WEEKS AGO MY AUNT CALLED ME A COMMUNIST. SHE'S MY
only aunt and I'm her only niece and, since we're both absolutely West Indian, the dialogue got pretty warm pretty fast.
Me? A Communist? I never even read one of those big-word
books on the subject. And I don't suppose I could easily tell a
Communist from a local Episcopalian unless he was wearing
one of those battery-operated buttons on his tie or, better yet,
if he happened to hang one of those little yellow signs inside
the back window of his powder blue BMW, you know, COM-
MUNIST ON BOARD! But the truth is I haven't ever seen anything
quite like that on the road, so far, and so I'm just not sure
exactly what my aunt's so exercised about. And I'm not so sure
she really knows, any more than I do, about this terrible
menace to everybody's backyard.

But her surprising accusation hurt me to the quick; I did
understand that she understood that everybody understands
that calling somebody a Communist is an entirely respectable,

This was the keynote address at the Activists' and Socialists' Conference at Hunter
College, New York, on December 5, 1986.

and popular, middle-class way to call somebody a low-down dirty dog.

This showdown between us began because we were talking by phone, the weekend just before Thanksgiving. Maybe you remember, that was the weekend when most of the whole wide world was trying to second-guess His Highness, the American king. And, meanwhile, His Highness was trying to figure out how the Pentagon could move the Bermuda Triangle to somewhere in the vicinity of Israel, Iran, and Nicaragua.

That was the weekend just before Thanksgiving—which would date the fateful conversation between me and my only aunt around four or five days before the *New York Times* finally published what so many folks were waiting to find out: Nancy Reagan's recipe for cornbread stuffing! I did study that recipe but then I decided against it because Miss Nancy started things off with a cornbread stuffing package mix and I don't hardly trust anything if I don't know how or why it got put together in a package, deal or no deal.

My aunt called me a Communist. So I got interested, of course: what did she mean by that?

a. She meant I was Crazy to even consider going to Nicaragua when, as far as she was concerned, I should naturally come over to her house and eat and eat and eat myself into a regulation state of traditional glut.

b. She meant I was crazy to contemplate anywhere else at all besides her very specific house for Thanksgiving dinner.

"What would you do down there, in Nicaragua?" she asked me. "Bring them shoes?"

I said I didn't think that was a bad idea.

She said, "But, that's a Communist country!"

I said, "No, it's Sandinista and the Communist party, in fact, only won a couple of seats in their national elections!"

My aunt snorted and she sneered: "*What* elections? Do you believe that propaganda?"

I asked her, "Do you believe that Ronald Reagan has lied, verifiably lied, about everything on earth *except* for Nicaragua—and on that particular subject he had this lapse and so he's told you the truth, the whole truth, and nothing but the truth?!"

My aunt adopted a warning tone of voice: "You're talking about the president!"

"I'm talking about a liar!"

"You're a Communist," my aunt repeated ominously.

"But, I've been to Nicaragua; I've seen that country for myself!"

"So what!" she countered.

"Are you saying that I necessarily know less about Nicaragua than you do precisely because I've been there and you've never been there but Ronald Reagan swears to you that Nicaragua's loading up a low-down missile base to barbecue the roses in your beautiful backyard?"

"You're a dupe of their propaganda," she retorted, complacently. "It's a matter of East and West; can't you see that?"

"East and West!" I exclaimed. "But if I got on a plane tomorrow, heading for Managua, I'd be flying south and west. West!"

"That's just geography!" My aunt was almost screaming now.

"But geography is not a matter of opinion," I said.

And here my aunt switched to her official Junior High School principal's voice.

"East and West," she patiently explained, "is a matter of ideology."

"Well," I said, "let's just say that we disagree."

"We don't disagree," she told me. "That's not the point. You're wrong! You're a Communist!"

(I, myself, was getting a little bit furious, in fact.)

"If I'm a Communist," I responded, "then most Americans

in this country are Communists because most Americans in this country do not support the president on Nicaragua!"

My aunt made no reply, so I continued: "If I'm a Communist, then there are Communist United States congressmen!"

"I wouldn't doubt it," she snapped back at me.

"And the Senate, the United States Senate: Do you realize that now a majority in the United States Senate will vote against Ronald Reagan's policies in Nicaragua?"

"What do I care about that!" she countered. "Four or five votes don't matter to me!"

"But that's majority rule!" I said.

"I don't care about majority rule," my aunt concluded. "I care about my country."

Well, I didn't go to Nicaragua last week and, to keep things perfectly balanced and perfectly clear, I didn't go to my aunt's house, either. But I have been thinking about my aunt and I have been thinking about whether or not I'm a Communist and I have been thinking more and more about His Highness, the American king, and I've been getting a little bit more than a little bit furious as the days go by.

Don't misunderstand me! I love my only aunt. And she is not a ridiculous woman. Nor is she inconsequential, evidently. And I would take anybody to the wall who dared to disrespect this elderly West Indian lady who has loved America so long until it's apparently possible that some larcenous Lady Clairol cowboy could come along and sell out the reality for a late-night movie. But:

1. I don't believe Ronald Reagan has a clue about communism any more than he knows where Managua is in relationship to Memphis, Tennessee. And my aunt needs to stop emulating an outstanding fool: just because you don't like something doesn't mean you should call it a Communist.

2. I personally am not about to call anybody or anything a

Communist because I wouldn't know what I'm talking about and because, unlike His Highness, the American king, I try to keep my mouth shut when I don't know what I'm talking about.

3. I am not mad about communism. I'm mad because people try to put me on the defensive by calling me this or that polysyllabic name nobody can really define.

4. I'm not worried about communism. I'm worried about my country: This is where I live. And what kind of situation do we have here where folks can claim ultra-loyalty to these United States, and where average Jane and average Joe can mouth a lot of "love it or leave it" mumbo jumbo and then turn around and tell you majority rule is beside the point?

5. I'm not worried about communism. I'm worried about my country! Is it really the case that a man can break United States law, international law, international treaties, is it really the case that a man—okay, a *white* man, but still—is it really the case that any man can disregard and dismiss the rulings of the World Court and, nevertheless, wave good-bye to 235 million children as he boards a helicopter for a weekend away from the consequeneces of his criminal misdeeds?

6. Is it happening in actual real life that one man can single-handedly erase and disgrace the Constitution of the United States and then expect to receive expressions of sympathy and support from leaders of something called the Democratic party?

7. Can it be true that facts, like geography, are no longer relevant to America? Is it agreed that a man can lie and lie and lie and then lie and then lie and then, nevertheless, occupy the highest office of the land?

8. Am I to believe that there's something wrong with giving water to someone who thirsts? Is there something wrong with giving peace to someone who petitions you for peace? Is there something wrong with giving shoes to somebody who doesn't

have shoes? Am I to believe that my country does not and will not respect the self-determining sovereign rights of any other country on the planet?

9. Should I accept that my country must, unerringly, endorse and bolster every tyrannous and evil force at large in the Third/the First World?

If the current setup shakes down to this, that I must *not* love the truth, that I must *not* want justice, that I must *not* allow other people to disagree with me, that I must *not* give a damn about the law, that I must *not* respect anybody different from my own peculiar image—or else I am a low-down dirty dog, then, yes: I am a low-down dirty dog! I am a Republican! I am a Boston Red Sox fan! I am a Communist! I am an angry West Indian poet!

And this is my country, this America. This is my home, this democracy. This is my steady hope, this slew-footed, knock-kneed, round-shouldered aggregate of querulous states agonizingly unified by the Declaration of Independence and the Constitution. I am not about to love a late-night movie perversion of my life. And I am not about to leave the reality of my rights.

At the end of the Freedom Summer of 1964, a great great lady, Mrs. Fannie Lou Hamer, traveled all the way from Mississippi to the Democratic convention in Atlantic City. She had just been beaten hideously in a southern jailhouse where they locked her up for urging Black Americans to register to vote. And as a member of the Mississippi Freedom Democratic Party, Mrs. Fannie Lou Hamer addressed our nation asking to have the MFDP seated in virtuous replacement of the regular racist delegation. You know how this story turns out: Lyndon Baines Johnson and his side-along sidekick, Walter Mondale, effectively prevented Mrs. Fannie from stating her full case to her compatriots coast to coast. And then the Democratic party chieftains offered what they termed a "compromise" of two seats to the Mississippi Freedom Democratic Party.

That great great lady, Mrs. Fannie Lou Hamer, do you know what she told them? She said, "We didn't come all the way up here for no two seats! When all of us is tired!"

And I wish you would embrace her words and her spirit as your own tonight. This is not the time to retreat or to compromise. You cannot compromise with truth. You cannot compromise with justice. You cannot compromise the Constitution of the United States with the hideous contradiction of an American king!

We did not come all the way up here for no two seats!

We want the whole thing: the intact legacy of the Declaration of Independence. Every single freedom guaranteed by the Constitution. A coherent foreign policy consistent with the principles of nonintervention and human rights. A judiciary and a congress at least equal to the office of the president. A president accountable to the people. A president who is not a pathological liar on a homicidal trip.

We need a president, not an American king.

We need a new president.

To save our country, we need an opposition party on the American scene.

Whether you call it Democratic or Rainbow or Socialist or Communist or Conservative, I truly don't care: we need an opposition party on the American scene. An opposition party that will burst forward, determined to win back our reasons for pride in these United States, an opposition party that will create an offensive against everything that is rotten and tyrannical and antidemocratic in our lives.

We need an opposition party that will send massive amounts of humanitarian aid to the Sandinistas in Nicaragua!

We need an opposition party that will send money and arms and advisers to the freedom-fighting African National Congress of South Africa!

We need an opposition party that will love and that will honor the citizens it begs to represent every whit as much as my aunt loves her larcenous Lady Clairol cowboy.

And why should we not have what we want?

Where are we and whose country is this, anyway?

Alternative Commencement Address at Dartmouth College, June 14, 1987

I FEEL TRULY PRIVILEGED BY YOUR INVITATION TO ME THAT makes possible my witness to this, your Alternative Commencement Ceremony, here, at Dartmouth College. In these American days of routine national dishonor and disgrace, in these American days of regular domestic cruelty and a deliberate, criminal exportation of terror abroad, it is something wonderful and fine to come among young Americans nevertheless believing in the exceptional, the virtuous potential of their lives, and of our country. To believe is to become what you believe. And so, you have become outstanding, alternative and virtuous in your faith. And as you have created yourselves in your chosen images of justice, independence, and courage, so have you altered and purified the mainstream in which you must live and grow.

None of your right conduct has been in vain. Not one of the wearisome meetings attended, not one of the risky postures assumed, not a single letter to the president, or statement of purpose, or telephone call, or tiring night of research in the library, will prove inconsequential, or mistaken. Every act committed because, with or without institutional support, you wish to rescue the world, and yourself, from the jeopardies of violence, hatred, and all systems of antidemocratic arrogance, every such act of righteous self-love will serve well the highest possibilities of human history.

And so I have come here to thank you for the bravery and the wisdom of your gifts to us. I have come here to join the American alternative that your proven faith and that your deeds have patiently and courageously composed.

I feel a very particular and fateful connection with the progressive community here at Dartmouth College. And let me tell you why. On my first visit to your campus, January 1986, I came to speak to you on the occasion of Dr. King's birthday. I flew here, direct from Atlanta, Georgia, where, for several days, Seven Stages Theatre had been auditioning a multiracial variety of young actors and actresses for the cast of *Bang Bang Uber Alles,* the musical drama for which I have written the lyrics and the libretto. Among the questions explored by *Bang Bang* are these: Can importantly different people—Black and white and gay and straight and romantically rivalrous and Latino and Jewish and poor and Ivy League somehow coalesce, despite their differences, and then, together, confront a common enemy? Or, can truly disparate persons soon enough perceive when the magnitude of an outside evil is greater than the deepest differences among them and, therefore, for their own collective good, unite to overcome that evil? In *Bang Bang Uber Alles,* the evil is the Ku Klux Klan. And the cast mainly consists of young singers and dancers who decide to challenge the Klan the way that they can: as performing artists who take their art into known Klan territory. Now, while myself and my collaborator, the musician-composer Adrienne Torf, met with imperturbably polite, respectful, and even excited response from the Black and white Southerners with whom we discussed our work, the firm consensus of biracial Atlanta was that the Klan represented a long-gone horror from another, earlier epoch. It might be useful and hopefully instructive to look back, as it were, on past racist and anti-Semitic and homophobic terrorist activities, yes, but the current, promising state of affairs could best be understood by the impending almost-nationwide observation of the birthdate of Dr. Martin Luther King, Jr. In Atlanta, itself, massive proud pageantry and rivers of rhetorical tribute to Dr. King's American dream poured into the streets, the schools, the churches, the civic auditoria, and onto the television screens. His dream had not died. The King of democratic love was alive. All was well, just about. And even as I walked around the Atlanta Memorial to Dr. King, and even as I did notice that it lay there, exposed to the public, a rectilinear concrete reflecting pool now empty of water, and even as I did notice the somewhat abandoned look of that humble shrine to his unerringly radical, his unerringly American ideals, I suddenly remembered my parents and how, were they alive, they would be astonished and fitful with pride. An almost-national holiday to honor a Black man! Certainly, a positive revolution had taken place between their generation and my own. The proper thing was, I thought, to pay attention to the great good news: huge changes of consciousness and conscience settling into place, as our new political reality.

And so, having cast most of the characters for *Bang Bang,* which would open in a world premiere production on June 12, I flew north to New Hampshire and Dartmouth, with my mind at ease, and a confident, hopeful heart. If so much good could replace so much evil in the South, what should I fear about this northern territory? True, I saw snow everywhere and, true, it was really cold outside and, true, the mountains of New Hampshire are, indeed, the White Mountains, but no matter, I was traveling up north to safety.

On my arrival, I found myself part of an enormous, exhilarated crowd of students, faculty, and administrators happily assembled for their Dartmouth celebration of the legacy of Dr. King. The large room in which we sat breathed simplicity, cleanliness, and goodwill. I heard no aggrieved and no accusatory tones of voice. I saw no conflict in that close-packed multiracial gathering. Trust and determination calmly controlled the atmosphere and modulated the proceedings. That evening, after the commemorative service, and after the reception and after the dinner after the reception, I took a measuring look around my quintessential Yankee quarters at the historic Hanover Inn. This frugality, this New England exactitude, this sturdy adherence to traditions as palpable as the spotless, flowered wallpaper or the tiny cake of Ivory soap, this was bedrock America, I thought, where I might find comfort and fall asleep, without fear.

The next morning, I arose quite early. It was cold. From my window, facing the Green, something seemed wrong. I could no longer clearly see the South African anti-apartheid shanties that Dartmouth students had erected there. Hurriedly, I dressed, packed, and went downstairs to the street. Across from me, at the intersection, a young white woman held up a crudely torn cardboard and magic marker sign: HONK IF YOU HATE APARTHEID. It was very cold. She must have been freezing. And she stood there, stubbornly lifting that sign above her head. It occurred to me that she might be crying. Something about the flush of her cheeks suggested that. One car after another car and then another car and then another car slowly passed by the student, in silence. Nobody hated apartheid. It occurred to me that I might be crying. I wanted to run anywhere: to stand there beside the student or really just to run away, away from Dartmouth, away from New Hampshire— or else towards the oncoming traffic and into it. I wanted to stop the cars with my body. I wanted every car in the United

States to raise an uproar. I wanted the horns of those cars to reach to Pretoria and shake down that infamy right there, right here, in Hanover, New Hampshire. But instead I stood still and I watched that young white woman and I listened and I waited until, finally, a car horn broke into that chill silence. And then another one, and then two cars honked their horns. I could hear them. I could see them. We were outnumbered but we were here.

A few minutes later, my hostess appeared in a great rush to drive me to the airport. On the way, she told me what had happened: she told me how on the very eve of Dartmouth's celebration of Dr. King, the teacher of nonviolence, the preacher of love and mercy, on that evening, twelve white students had smashed apart the anti-apartheid shanties because, they said, they found them unsightly, they found them an aesthetic disfigurement of the center town where they planned to convene the annual festivities of Winter Carnival. Those twelve disciples of pure white snow could not tolerate those shanties. They could not and would not abide by civilized rules of conflict. They felt no shame. They knew no reasons for restraint. In New Hampshire, one of the few states to reject Martin Luther King, Jr., Day as a legal holiday, those disciples had no need to worry about repercussions: they were safe. Their violence against those pitiful stick shacks spawned by apartheid was safe violence: only the victims would be hurt. The perpetrators of that violence would go unharmed or, as in the notable instance of Bernhard Goetz, might even attract acclaim.

I will admit to you that I was shocked: The Dartmouth smashing of the shanties pierced me like an arrowhead of ice. How could such disregard for suffering, how could such disrespect for American freedom of dissent, how could such derisive, brutal effrontery arise among such young Americans of so much privileged education? What had they been learning anyway? And who was teaching it to them? How could the venerable institution of Dartmouth College persist with its investment in South Africa? What is the excuse?

I understand that a Reverend Eleazer Wheelock founded Dartmouth College in 1769; it was his intention to enlighten "the Indians" and other youth with Christian precepts. Noting that the Native American population of New Hampshire is currently too infinitesimal to be listed in the *World Almanac* of today, and noting that nowhere in the entire state of New Hampshire will you even find a Native American reservation, I would have to wonder about the substance of that enlightenment. Or, as Frederick Douglass wrote in the appendix to his *Narrative of the Life of Frederick Douglass, an American Slave:*

Between the Christians of this land, and the Christianity of Christ, I recognize the widest possible difference—so wide, that to receive the one as good, pure, and lovely, is of necessity to reject the other as bad, corrupt, and wicked. To be the friend of the one, is of necessity to be the enemy of the other. I love the pure, peaceable, and impartial Christianity of Christ: I therefore hate the corrupt, slaveholding, women-whipping, cradle-plundering, partial hypocritical Christianity of this land.

Let me put it to you this way: What is the Christian precept that justifies collaboration with South Africa? Why does Dartmouth College refuse to divest? And what is the meaning of the *quote* Indian *unquote* head that appears as the visual logo for this school? Is it a memorial cartoon? Is it a macabre memento of a hunting trip? On January 7, 1986, I left New Hampshire with a checkmate of opposite feelings. My best hopes about America had been confirmed. And my worst fears had been revived.

And then, exactly one year ago today, on June 14, 1986, in Atlanta, Georgia, the Ku Klux Klan came to the parking lot behind the Seven Stages Theatre. In full Klan regalia, ranging from black satin robes and headdress to Marine combat outfits to white silk sheets, several carloads of Klansmen got out of their cars and began their attempt to shut down *Bang Bang Uber Alles*. Late that afternoon, the director had received an anonymous call telling him that the Klan would materialize at 6:30 P.M. But no one, especially not the Atlanta police, had taken the call seriously. In fact, the local precinct grudgingly sent only two police officers to the theater, "just in case." Six-thirty came and went. The actors, the band, the director, the choreographer, Adrienne Torf, and myself, we were all there, standing around. The police lounged about, laughing and saying that obviously the call had been a practical joke. My gut suggested otherwise; I didn't suppose punctuality, or any other virtue, to be part of Klan code. At ten minutes to seven, a friend of the production raced into the theater lobby, eyes wide. "Lock the door!" he shouted. "They're here! They're here!" I can't remember precisely what happened, minute by minute, after that. It was too wild, and terrifying. The police ordered us to stay inside. But most of us could not resist this alarming opportunity for face-to-face contact with the evil we had been writing and singing and acting against. When I did manage to reach the edge of the parking lot, I could scarcely glimpse the Ku Klux Klan. It seemed that more than a hundred Atlanta policeman occupied the entire space. In addition, television crews from all of the networks had set up their cameras and microphones in a big competitive jumble. In addition, neighborhood residents, most of them white, were crowding around the Klansmen, yelling obscenities and, apparently, furious about this menacing invasion.

I could hear it. I could see it. We were there and, this time, "we" outnumbered "them."

Forty-five minutes after their arrival, and warning that they would return, the Ku Klux Klan withdrew. After they left, the police sergeant called the cast and the band onstage and told them it was probable that the Klan would come back; they might firebomb the theatre and/or assault the actors and musicians and, so, there was a choice to be made. If they quit, the sergeant said, that would give to the Klan a victory: the Klan would have succeeded in intimidating them, and closing down the show. But, yes, it was dangerous. He could promise them police protection for the remainder of the five-week run. But, yes, it was dangerous. What did the cast and the band want to do? They answered, those young performing artists in Atlanta, they responded by saying that they wanted to do vocal warm-ups and get on with it.

We have survived a fearsomely long year since that hot southern night in Atlanta, when previously apolitical singers and dancers became American heroes, not unlike yourselves. During those twelve months, our country has apparently become inured to constitutional violation, executive deceit, and ominous hysteria. We have suffered the criminal likes of Ollie North offered to us as an exemplary patriot. But we have also become aware—belatedly—of the painstaking good works of twenty-seven-year-old Benjamin Linder, a mechanical engineer from Seattle. At the moment of his murder by the contras, Benjamin Linder was measuring the water pressure of a stream in northern Nicaragua; he was testing it to determine its capacity as a source for hydroelectric power. Most of Nicaragua still lacks electricity.

Ollie North—Lieutenant Colonel Oliver North, self-proclaimed super-patriot and aide to the National Security Council, who flagrantly broke the law on behalf of Nicaraguan contras—versus Benjamin Linder: It would seem that there is even a dialectical unfolding of American destiny and impact. All of us know about the Ku Klux Klan in Forsyth County, Georgia. But many of us may have forgotten that the second march for brotherhood reversed the odds: Once again, we were there and, that second time, "we" outnumbered "them."

I know that we, the people of these United States, have grown up from an elitist group of self-selected, affluent white men into the duly entitled, heterogeneous population of 235 million Americans that we constitute, because we, the people, have insisted on that revolutionary growth. We have not been quiet or obedient. We have not cooperated with domestic tyranny any more than we have ever willingly submitted to a foreign tyrant. We have had to fight and we have had civil wars. We have sat down, stood up, linked arms, blocked the doorways, broken the windows, prayed, chanted, registered, gone underground, gone out on strike, or battled our way into public office. We, the heterogeneous peoples of these United States, we embody the unruly, demanding, visionary reasons why the Constitution of 1787 had to be amended by the Bill of Rights in 1791. The Founding Fathers quite entirely neglected to include the rights of any of the citizens they planned to govern. Hence, the First Amendment, Article One, reads as follows: "Congress shall make no law respecting an establishment of religion, or prohibiting the free exercise thereof; or abridging the freedom of speech, or of the press; or the right of the people peaceably to assemble, and to petition the Government for a redress of grievances." Think of it: *That was an amendment,* an afterthought to the Constitution! It is we, the governed, who insisted on those first ten amendments and it is we, the otherwise ungovernable, who have caused the ensuing sixteen amendments to become our national laws.

And why should that founding document require so many amendments? The Fourteenth Amendment begins as follows: "All persons born or naturalized in the United States, and subject to the jurisdiction thereof, are citizens of the United States and of the State wherein they reside. No State shall make or enforce any law which shall abridge the privileges or immunities of citizens of the United States; nor shall any State deprive any person of life, liberty, or property, without due process of law; nor deny to any person within its jurisdiction the equal protection of the laws."

What more could any one of us want, or need? The Fourteenth Amendment equally entitles each of us to the full significance of American citizenship. Right? Well, it should, but because Article One of the Constitution excludes all women, and Native Americans, and any white residents of America who might not be free (e.g., indentured servants), from the Founders' concept of "person," and because African-Americans are defined as "three-fifths of all other persons," it becomes clear that the touchstone to American democracy is the question: Who is a Person? Or, who are the people?

In 1782, nine years before the ratification of the Bill of Rights, *Letters from an American Farmer* by St. Jean de Crèvecoeur became available and they enjoyed great popularity among those Americans who could read. In the third letter, "What is an American?," we find these ideas: "What then is the American, this new man? He is either a European, or the descendant of a European. . . . He is an American, who, leaving behind him all his ancient prejudice and manners, receives new ones from the new mode of life he has embraced, the new government he obeys, and the new rank he holds. . . . Here, individuals of all nations (i.e., English men, Dutch men, French men) are melted into a new race of men." And, further on, de Crèvecoeur expands: "No sooner does a European arrive, no matter what condition, than his eyes are opened upon the fair prospect; he beholds hardly any poor; he seldom hears of punishments and executions and he wonders at the elegance of our towns, those miracles of industry and freedom."

This was the popular, powerful consciousness of the governors of America, immediately following the American Revolution.

But perhaps we should not be surprised by such forthright confessions of a complacent ruling egotism. Here are three historical items that logically precede or else ensue from such a clearly American perspective. This is an excerpt from the Pilgrim governor William Bradford's account of the Pequot War in 1637:

And those that first entered found sharp resistance from the enemy (i.e. the Indians) who both shot at and grappled with them; others ran into their houses and brought out fire and set them on fire . . . and thereby more were burnt to death than was otherwise slain: it burnt their bowstrings and made them unserviceable. Those that escaped the fire were slain with the sword, some hewed to pieces, others run through with their rapiers and very few escaped. It was conceived they thus destroyed about 400 at this time. It was a fearful sight to see them thus frying in the fire and the streams of blood quenching the scene, and horrible was the stink and scent thereof; but the victory seemed a sweet sacrifice, and they gave praise thereof to God, who had wrought so wonderfully for them, thus to their enemies in their hands and give them so speedy a victim over so proud and insulting an enemy.

Listen, please, to item number two:

Benjamin Abbot gave his testimony that last March was a twelve month, this carrier was very angry with him, upon laying out some land near her husband's: her expressions in this anger were that she would stick as close to Abbot as the bark stuck to the tree: and that he should repent of it afore seven years came to an end. . . . Presently, after this, he was taken with a swelling in his foot, and then with a pain in his sides, and exceedingly tormented. . . . Sarah Abbot, also his wife testified that her husband was not only all this while afflicted in his body, but also that strange, extraordinary and unaccountable calamities befell his cattle. . . .

Unfortunately, this is literal testimony from the Salem witch trials of 1692, as reported by Cotton Mather (an illustrious Harvard graduate). At the conclusion of those trials, nineteen people were hanged, most of them women, and one man was pressed "by heavy stone" to death.

Here is item number three:

My mother and I were separated when I was but an infant before I knew her as my mother. It is a common custom, in the part of Maryland from which I ran away, to part children from their mothers at a very early age.

I never saw my mother, to know her as such, more than four or five times in my life, and each of these times was very short in duration, and at night. She was hired by a Mr. Stewart, who lived about 12 miles from my home. She made her journeys to see me in the night, travelling the whole distance on foot, after the performance of her day's work. She was a field hand, and whipping is the penalty for not being in the field at sunrise. . . . I do not recollect of ever seeing my mother by the light of day. She was with me in the night. She would lie down with me, and get me to sleep, but long before I waked she was gone. Very little communication ever took place between us. Death soon ended what little we could have while she lived, and with it her hardships and suffering. She died when I was about 7 years old, on one of my master's farms, near Lee's hill. I was not allowed to be present during her illness, at her death, or burial.

That last comes from *Narrative of the Life of Frederick Douglass, an American Slave.*

"What is an American?" *He* was not supposed to be an Indian. *He* was not supposed to be a *she.* He was not supposed to be Black or the African-American descendant of slaves. And yet, here we are, at our own indomitable insistence, here we are, the peoples of America.

I hope it will help the fortitude of your rebellion against evil to know, and to understand, that our collective history as Americans is not the history of a paradise lost. Rather ours is the history of a democratic republic under torturous but steadfast construction. Extreme challenges to our democracy abound around us. But let us recognize these attacks upon our honorable heritage of mostly infamous heroines and heroes for what they are: attacks upon the basis for the liberty and the well-being of all of our lives. We cannot permit any one of us to slip outside the covenant of the Fourteenth Amendment to the Constitution. Every American, be she indigent or elderly or disabled, every

American, be he Black or Hispanic or Native American or White or homosexual, every American be he be she the president of these United States or the begging body that hides at dawn must be bound by the law of our country that, in turn, shall entitle him or her to the awesomely powerful privileges of American citizenship.

Once we exclude any human being from political and social status as our equal, our compatriot, once we befoul our mouths with phrases such as three-fifths of anything whatsoever, once we defile this generous earth with proposals for preventive detention or mandatory testing or quarantine or concentration camps, we forswear our own, always tenuous, always contingent, prospects for freedom.

Quite simply we do not need preemptive strike capabilities: we need preventive medicine. We do not need arms for the contras: we need housing for the homeless. We do not need Ollie North: we need Benjamin Linder. We need women and men who will bend down to the waters of a stream and test those waters for their humane usefulness. We need artists who will declaim and dance and sing against the Ku Klux Klan. We need students who will hate apartheid more than they love the delights of a Winter Carnival. We need women and men to rebuild the collapsing bridges of America. We need women and men to legislatively interdict the skip-town habits of national industries. We need an alternative family refuge for our runaway children who either disappear or stay home and drug themselves into oblivion.

And even here, in this beautiful, pristine state of New Hampshire, even here where the forests and the lakes and the villages of such obvious grace wait, vulnerable under the shadow of the chances for an accident at the Seabrook nuclear reactor, and especially here, on this splendidly kept campus of Dartmouth College where the unsightly anti-apartheid shanties have been removed from sight, especially here where homophobia and racism and sexism persist but where you have actively defied each one of those evil barriers to a free life, especially here at this Alternative Commencement Ceremony, especially here do I believe that we, the people, will find the humane, educated, American leadership, and rescue, that we need, and that even the most hateful among us deserve.

I hold this belief because you have mounted your beginning struggle for a democratic life where you have found yourself—which is where you belong: This is your country! This is your college!

And, boldly or not, you have dared to enliven the dialectical unfolding of our common American destiny.

So it does seem to me that you have been well educated! In his *Democratic Vistas,* Walt Whitman recalls the words of a librarian of Congress who wrote, in 1869: "The true question to ask, respecting a book, is, *has it helped any human soul?*"

Evidently, some of the books that you have studied here have been good books: they have tutored your soul with an inclination towards kindness and with an ineradicable longing for justice!

I look upon your faces, now, at this commencement of the rest of your adult American lives and I see the flower of this state, the purple lilac, rising delicate and lovely from the granite of our difficult but yielding American situation.

And your faith encourages my own.

I thank you from my heart. And I extend to you my deepest congratulations and good wishes.

INSIDE AMERICA:

''My Perfect Soul Shall Manifest Me Rightly''

An Essay on Blackfolks and the Constitution

THERE IS A TERRIBLE TROUBLE ACROSS THE LAND. OUR NA-tional security no longer rests upon good housing, wholesome food, and excellence of education. Our national industries no longer provide dependable high-pay employment for millions of workers. Our national budget every year shrinks its commit-ment to the environmental and health-care support that our human survival, as citizens, demands. The president believes he has become an American king, accountable to neither man nor law. The courts increasingly rule against the rights of the accused, the unpopular, the weak. And the Congress vacillates between inertia and compulsive compromise.

As a nation we have become a beacon for tyrants, greed-driven entrepreneurs, and militaristic fantasies. As a people we have become accustomed to the homeless, the beggars, the terrorized minorities, and the terrified elderly. As an electorate, we have become the craven subjects of deceitful, lawless, and inhumane leadership. As African-Americans, we have become coast-to-coast targets for resurgent racist insolence and injury.

There is a terrible trouble across the land. It would seem that Lincoln's call for a democracy or, more precisely, his Gettysburg appeal for a "government of the people, by the people, and for the people" has failed to win the willing allegiance of an American majority. But that is not the case. The Gettysburg Address remains the most beloved of all American manifestos. But we have yet to experience majority rule in these United States. From the days of the Thirteen Colonies when any white man wishing to compete for public office or to vote for any of the candidates had to possess baronial amounts of money and/or land to qualify, from those days to these, when the importance of any public office directly correlates to the enormous sums of money a candidate must either possess or else control for his ready disposal, we do not have "majority rule." If we did, for example, the majority of the people—women—would not still struggle for equal rights. Nor would we witness the verified disjuncture of most of the electorate opposed to U.S. policies in Central America and South Africa while those policies continue, unperturbed by "the will of the people."

Democracy was never the goal of the Founding Fathers. "The richest man in America," George Washington, and his autocratic, slaveholding comrades wanted political autonomy for themselves and a comfortable continuation of their elitist wealth and privilege, here, in the New World. Indeed, most of the Fathers of America occupied public positions of power under the British. These white men were not egalitarians or rebels for justice!

In 1776, Thomas Jefferson (the "owner" of several hundred slaves) penned the Declaration of Independence, which begins:

"We hold these Truths to be self-evident, that all Men are created equal, that they are endowed by their Creator with certain unalienable Rights, that among these are Life, Liberty, and the Pursuit of Happiness—That to secure these rights, Governments are instituted among Men, deriving their just Powers from the Consent of the Governed." But Jefferson did not suppose "Men" to include anyone significantly different from himself: a white male aristocrat. And, in fact, that same Declaration elsewhere complains that King George "has excited domestic Insurrections" (slave rebellions) and, also, incited the "merciless Indian Savages" (Native Americans opposed to their own extermination).

There is a terrible trouble across the land, in part, because we were never the "Men": and because we were never the People: We were never the intended beneficiaries of the Founding Fathers of the Founding Documents of America.

And when the Constitution of 1787 came before the "Fathers" for ratification, there was literally no reason why any of those self-selected patriarchs should vote against it: the Constitution simply sets forth the procedure whereby the powerful shall rule the People. It provides guideline mechanics for the governing of the republic of America: how senators shall be elected and on what basis of apportionment, and so forth. In addition, therein lies the ratified design for the American system of "checks and balances" whereby no one of the three chambers of national government (presidential/congressional/judicial) shall overrule the others.

Underlying these procedures were two major concerns: that the chief executive not become in any sense a monarch, and that federal authority should hold, absolute, over all of the territories of those uniting States. And, underlying the consent of the "Fathers" to the Constitution was a prophetic compromise between the North and the South: In exchange for Constitutional protection of the slave trade and the property rights of

Southerners, the North would receive constitutional protection for its capitalist control over trade and commerce.

"We the People of the United States," the opening phrase of the Constitution, did not allude to the majority of white men, nor to any women, nor to "Indians," nor to the African "three-fifths of all other Persons." In short, the 1787 Founding Document did not represent, or even contemplate, most of the human beings alive in America, at that time!

The Fathers of America were not our fathers! They would have been astounded by the very notion of familial relationship to any of us! And yet we came among them and we did not perish. Indeed, the irreducible difference of our African-American lives has tested, has clarified, has cleansed and, finally, has altered the entire body politic to which we now belong. Seventy years after the signing of the Constitution, the moral treacheries inherent in that document, the invidious compromise at the root of this republic, became wantonly apparent. One of our true forefathers, a former slave, Dred Scott, petitioned the courts for his freedom.

In the Dred Scott Decision of 1857, the United States Supreme Court ruled that slaves, by definition, were not citizens and that property rights (in this instance, the alleged constitutional rights of slaveowners) should prevail over any other alleged constitutional rights.

We were not the Men. We were never the People. We were bought and sold and judged as property, *as things*. And from that Dred Scott ruling down to the "Baby M" case of 1987, the constitutional enshrinement of property rights versus human or civil rights remains a staining, structural ambivalence, at best: an amoral invitation to democratic crisis among conflicting needs or interests.

And yet this is the Founding Document on which our status, and much of our destiny, here, depends: this tricky, conflicted, noble and ignoble starter tablet of laws that, as the first Black

Supreme Court justice, Thurgood Marshall, has remarked, required "several amendments, a civil war, and momentous social transformation to attain the system of constitutional government, and its respect for the individual freedoms and human rights, we hold as fundamental today."

Consider this brief history: Four years after the signing of the Constitution, the Fathers adopted the first ten amendments, "The Bill of Rights." These amendments introduced into America the concepts and the issues of the rights of those governed, the People: freedom of religion/freedom of speech/ trial by jury, and so forth. But, again, "the People" did not include most of the white, let alone any of the African, inhabitants of America. That was 1791. Much later on, these further amendments to the Constitution tell their own lifetimes of embattlement:

1865: The Thirteenth Amendment abolishes slavery (78 years after the signing of the Constitution)

1868: The Fourteenth Amendment confers citizenship upon all persons born or naturalized within the United States and stipulates "equal protection under the law"

1870: The Fifteenth Amendment grants to Black men the right to vote

1920: The Nineteenth Amendment (132 years after the signing of the Constitution) grants to women the right to vote

1964: The Twenty-Fourth Amendment abolishes the poll tax, or payment of any tax, as a prerequisite to the right to vote (thereby abolishing wealth/property as a criterion of eligibility for the right to vote: 1964!)

Nevertheless, and despite our emerging, tortuous, constitutional inclusion inside that mythical, that democratic circle of the People, did we not, did we not have to, wage a Civil Rights Revolution, here in America, more than 170 years after the signing of the Founding Documents? And, did we not, did we not have to, turn this country around, on and off international microphones and cameras, and risk multitudes, and sacrifice far too many known and unknown heroic children and women and men—warriors for our civil rights, our "equal protection under the law"?

And are we, now, safe?

And are we, now, free?

And is the Ku Klux Klan and Howard Beach and Bernhard Goetz a paranoid construction of our idling, victim minds? And are we hallucinating or has Ronald Reagan declared himself above the laws he was sworn to uphold and, therefore, has he become the first American king? And is it true or false that this King Reagan's arrogation and exercise of illegal powers in contempt of congressional law violates the basic balance of powers decreed by the Constitution? And has the United States Supreme Court recently challenged essential constitutional rights by validating the death penalty and by inaugurating "preventive detention"? And have we fallen asleep or is there truly no huge outcry to halt and reverse these profound erosions of our elusive constitutional protections against tyranny?

And is it merely our imaginings or do the inhumanities of a profit-and-power-obsessed economy first, and worst, assault the last of us to enter the fully entitled circle of the People: women, African-Americans, Native Americans, Latino-Americans, and the poor of America, per se?

There is a terrible trouble across the land. There is great uncertainty of purpose. There is very little faith. And our ignorance of power—*why* it happens that some have while others have not/*when* power can change hands or move from the few to the many/*how* we may easily lose what we have gained with so much difficulty—this ignorance among us grows more dangerous, day by day! Nothing that we have was given to us. Anything that we may hope to claim or boast

about or stand upon, here, in these United States of mixed-up/
contradictory America is something our true mothers and fathers purchased at the non-negotiable price of their own
heart's ease. *Easy and ease:* they gave that up, shouting aloud
or on their knees, because they believed that ceaseless, faithful
agitation and that deliberate sacrifice would secure for us, their
children, what they must only ponder and pursue.

But now we are no longer children. Now we can know and
must see, rightly, the truth of our predicament: It is they, the
powerful few, who have never been the People. It is they, the
would-be ruler aristocrats of politics and commerce, who composed those Founding Documents that value property as much
as or more than human life, and it is they who have dared to
evaluate other human beings as things for hire or for sale. It is
they, the powerful few, who make laws without our consent,
and then it is they who break the laws, with evident impunity.
It is they, the arrogant governors of our national life, who rush
to wars that they, themselves, refuse to fight; instead they draft
our sons and daughters into an unjustifiable, military death. It
is they, the cowardly, lying, mean, egomaniacal, and irrepressi-
bly avaricious ruling elite who invent and promulgate the
ideology and the practice of racism, throughout the world.

Just as slavery established the concept of certain human
beings as subhuman or "three-fifths," or *things,* racism maintains that certain human beings do not qualify as People.
Therefore, certain human beings may be rightfully denied their
land, their life, their liberty, and their pursuit of happiness.
Once this ideology takes root, once it becomes accepted that
any man may categorize any other man or woman as less than
he is/less than a human being, then every man and every
woman becomes a possible *thing* that must prove "itself"
useful or useless/necessary or dispensable to the lunatics making such judgments: multinational magnates who "decide"

whether or not they will move their manufacturing plants from Detroit to the Philippines, or the five-star generals sitting in front of the master switch to nuclear annihilation.

There is a terrible trouble across the land because We, the People, are becoming more powerful. Despite the limited intentions of the Fathers of this republic, We, the People of America, are forcing a democracy out of Pilgrim Rock: questions of equality and human rights reverberate in public discussions of domestic and foreign policy, alike. This was not always the case. This was not meant to be.

And the disease of racist ideology is losing its evil force. More and more white Americans realize that we, African-Americans, are not the ones who pollute the water or sell our national parks or threaten social security or reduce federal college loans or erase public subsidies for housing or truck nuclear wastes through the streets of their cities. And, conversely, we, the objects of racist hatred, both here and throughout the Third World, exhibit less and less tolerance for racist exploitation and abuse, less and less willingness to tolerate even one more day without the means to our full dignity and freedom.

We, the People, are becoming the powerful! For one real moment in this bicentennial year of celebration for the Constitution, the Reverend Jesse Jackson was proclaimed the certified front-runner for the Democratic candidacy for the presidency of these United States!

But we are not yet safe.

But we are not yet free.

And, yes, there is a terrible trouble across the land because power does not change hands, power does not transfer from the pockets of a calculating elite into the treasury of the common good without a mighty, tightening resistance to such change!

And if we shall reach our safety in this place, then we shall not forget the centuries of collective agitation/the seismic/ secretive/home-based/coalitional and worldwide/persevering bravery that made even the privileges of our current peril a remarkable possibility: WE ARE NOW THE PEOPLE. And it is for us to decide whether or not democracy/a "government of the people, by the people, and for the people" shall undergird this "new birth of freedom" or else "perish from the earth."

It is for us, the living, to ensure that We the People shall become the powerful. We must swiftly secure a much more comprehensive and a much more accurate representation of our needs and viewpoints at every level of American government, up to and including the presidency. We must discover or become our own candidates. We must join or become the unified electorate that will win every election we enter, from sheriff to mayor to United States senator. We cannot do this alone. But we need not struggle without allies. We have become as fully entitled, as every other citizen, and more fully at risk: We are the People; we have entered the magical, democratic circle of our own collective undertaking. And we must believe that many other Americans will gladly join us there. Because they will. Because they have.

You could sometimes scream from the weight of the hatred our lives must overcome: you could sometimes wish we could walk quietly away from all of that. Sometimes it seems too much too long too deeply tearing at the vitals of our pride. But we have made a journey through a wilderness and, along the hardship road, we have kept our inner civilizing peace: we have infiltrated the barbarians around us; we have gathered converts to our side or we have forced our enemies to pretend, to progressively enact, the righteous legislation required for our common good. We have made our journey through a wilderness and, at last, we stand our ground. We are saying, "I am here and it is here '*I must be found. . . . my perfect soul shall manifest me rightly.*' "[1]

---

[1] *Othello,* act 1, scene 2, lines 30–32.

DON'T YOU TALK ABOUT MY MOMMA!

WHEN I WAS GROWING UP, THE ONE SURE TRIGGER TO A DOWN-and-out fight was to say something—anything—about somebody's mother. As a matter of fact, we refined things, eventually, to the point where you didn't have to get specific. All you had to do was push into the face of another girl or boy and, close as you could, almost nose to nose, just spit out the two words: "Your mother!" This item of our code of honor was not negotiable and, clearly, we took it pretty seriously: even daring to refer to someone's mother put you off-limits. From the time you learned how to talk, everybody's momma remained the holiest of the holies. Yes, we were young. And a lot of people probably thought we were hoodlums, or something like that. But we knew we were smart: we made and kept ourselves ready to deal on those dangerous streets. Many of us, there, in Bedford-Stuyvesant, were poor. But very few of us

This was a keynote address for the Williams College Conference on the Black Family in February 1987.

were stupid. You couldn't be. In those days, as now, Black kids enjoyed damned little margin for error.

So we never lost track. We could feel it. We could see it. We could hear it. We could not deny it. And we did not ever forget it, this fact, that the first the last and the most, that the number one persevering, resourceful, resilient, and devoted person in our lives was, and would always be, your mother and my mother.

But sometimes, you know, we grow up without growing wise. Sometimes we become so sophisticated we have to read the *New York Times* in order to figure out whether it's a hot or a rainy day. We read the fine print in order to find out the names of our so-called leaders. We defer to erstwhile experts on the subject of sex. And we watch so much television that we can no longer tell the difference between a president who loves his—which is to say, *this*—country and a president who freely violates the Constitution. But what truly surprises me is Black-folks listening to a whole lot of white blasphemy against Black feats of survival, Blackfolks paying attention to people who never even notice us except to describe us as "female-headed" or something equally weird. (I would like to know, for a fact, has anybody ever seen a female-headed anything at all? What did it look like? What did it do? Could you buy or marry one of them?) On the subject of language, let me briefly register my further unhappiness with the phrase "the feminization of pov-erty." The millions of human beings that lamentable phrase hopes to describe will never agree that poverty is feminine or that they, themselves, participate in the invention of the tor-tures of poor women in America. Nor will impoverished Black women of America willingly submit to the flagrantly popular, illogical, and misogynist response suggesting that the solution to the impoverishment of Black women/Black mothers is the enablement of everybody else. We know that most Black chil-dren now live in Black families headed by Black women. And

DON'T YOU TALK ABOUT MY MOMMA!

we know that the most punishing poverty fastens itself to women, per se, and to Black women, always. I submit, therefore, that we also know, in our right minds, that Black women and Black mothers require specific, immediate, programmatic rescue! I mean, if somebody is suffering hunger, then it is she who needs the food.

Now, I am not opposed to sophistication, per se, but when you lose touch with your momma, when you take the word of an absolute, hostile stranger over and above the unarguable truth of your own miraculous, hard-won history, and when you don't remember to ask, again and again, "Compared to what?" I think you don't need to worry about enemies anymore. You better just worry for yourself.

Back in 1965, Daniel P. Moynihan issued a broadside insult to the National Black Community. With the full support of a Democratic administration that was tired of Negroes carrying on about citizenship rights, and integration, and white racist violence, Moynihan came through with the theory that we, Blackfolks, and that we, Black women, in particular, constituted "the problem." It was not the failure of the United States federal and local governments to equally entitle and equally protect all of its citizens, but it was the failure of Black families to resemble the patriarchal setup of White America that explained our unequal, segregated, discriminated-against, and violently hated Black experience of nondemocracy, here. We were, he said, a problem. We were, he said, a pathological culture. Moynihan said these things while white patriarchal America was proving itself to the world in a needless savagery of resistance to our nationwide movement for justice, that's all: just justice.

And I wrote and published this little poem, for Mr. Moynihan, back then:

MEMO TO DANIEL PRETTY MOYNIHAN

You done what you done
I do what I can

Don't you liberate me
from my female black pathology

I been working off my knees
I been drinking what I please

And when I vine
I know I'm fine
I mean
All right for each and every
  Friday night

But you been screwing me so long
I got a idea something's wrong
with you

I got a simple proposition
You take over my position

Clean your own house, babyface.

That's all he deserved, as I saw it. I couldn't take him seriously, and certainly not to *my* heart! Plus, I didn't have the time for Mr. Moynihan or any other Mr. Man's theories about me. I was busy. I was going to meetings. I was demonstrating outside Chock Full o' Nuts. I was going to work. I was raising my son. (Did that make me or my child or both of us a female-headed whatchamacallit?) I had no time to waste.

And, besides, back then, you didn't bring your enemies into your house: you confronted them on the sidewalks, or in court, or on the floor of Congress. But when you went home, you went home to family. Of course, that meant that you had a family. It might not look like Dick and Jane or Ronald and Nancy but it surely did for you what the White House has never done for Black people: our family took care of us, and helped us to keep on keeping on. Our families might have adult women and children, and no adult men, or our families might have one white parent and one Black parent, and their children, or our families might have three generations living in two rooms, or our families might have, and, back then, as now, the majority did have, a Black father and a Black mother and their children, but regardless, we were all there, for each other when we came home. And we, the people of this allegedly "pathological ghetto culture," we were waging the most principled, unassailably moral revolution of the twentieth century: we, the pathological community of Blackfolks were forcing these United States to finally honor the democratic promises responsible for the First American Revolution.

And, in the meantime, how was the dominant, the intact patriarchal white culture of America, how was the allegedly nonpathogenic but, nevertheless, racist and sexist culture of white America responding to this, the Civil Rights Revolution? By blowing up the 16th Street Baptist Church in Birmingham, September 15, 1963. By murdering four Black girls who had gone there for Sunday school. Or, in 1965, by murdering the unarmed white minister, Reverend James Reeb, in Selma. And, as well, in 1965, by publishing The Moynihan Report.

So, no, I didn't take him, or any of my enemies, to heart. But now there are Black voices joining the choruses of the absurd. There are national Black organizations and purported Black theoreticians who have become indistinguishable from verified enemies of Blackfolks in this country. These sophisticated Black voices jump to page one of the delighted, ultra-reliable *New York Times* because they are willing to be misinterpreted and to lament and defame the incredible triumph of Black women, the victory of Black mothers that is the victory of our continuation as a people in America. Archly delivering jargon phrases about "the collapse of Black family structure" and "the destructive culture of poverty in the ghetto" and, of course, "the crisis of female-headedness," with an additional screaming reference to "the shame of teenage pregnancy," these Black voices come to us as the disembodied blatherings of peculiar offspring: Black men and women who wish to deny the Black mother of their origins and who wish to adopt white Daniel P. Moynihan as their father. I happen to lack the imagination necessary to forgive, or understand, this phenomenon. But the possible consequences of this oddball public outcry demand our calm examination.

According to these new Black voices fathered by Mr. Moynihan, it would seem that the Black family subsists in a terrible, deteriorating state. That's the problem. The source for the problem is the Black Family (i.e., it's not White; it suffers from female-headedness). The solution to the Black Family Problem is, you guessed it, the Black Family. It must, itself, become more white—more patriarchal, less female-headed, more employed more steadily at better and better-paying jobs.

Okay?

Not okay. My own assessment of that analysis proceeds as follows:

Number One. The Black Family persists despite a terrible deteriorating state of affairs prevailing in these United States. This is a nation unwilling and progressively unable to provide for the well-being of most of its citizens: our economic system increasingly concentrates our national wealth in the hands of fewer and fewer interest groups. Our economic system increasingly augments the wealth of the richest sector of the citizenry while it diminishes the real wages and the available livelihood of the poor. Our economic system refuses responsibility for the equitable sharing of national services and monies among its various peoples. Our economic system maintains an unmistakable commitment to a Darwinian pseudophilosophy of laissez-faire. Our economic system remains insensitive to the political demands of a democracy and, therefore, our economic system does not yield to the requirements of equal entitlement vis-à-vis women, children, Black men, Hispanic Americans, Native

Americans, the elderly, and the disabled. If you total those
American people you have an obvious majority of Americans
squeezed outside the putative benefits of "free enterprise." Our
economic system continues its building, trillion-dollar commitment *not* to the betterment of the lives of its citizens but,
rather, to the development and lunatic replication of a mili-
tary-industrial complex. In this context, then, the Black Family
persists, yes, in a terrible deteriorating state. But we did not
create this state. Nor do we control it. And we are not suffering
"collapse." Change does not signify collapse. The nuclear,
patriarchal family structure of White America was never our
own; it was not *African*. And, when we arrived to slavery,
here, why or how should we emulate the overseer and the
master, we who amounted to three-fifths of a human being, we
who could, by law, neither marry nor retain our children
against the predation of the slave economy? Nonetheless, from
under the whip through underpaid underemployment, and
worse, Black folks have formulated our own family, our own
home base for nurture and for pride. We have done this from
extended kinship methods of taking care to teenagers thrilled,
not appalled, by the prospect of a child: a Black child. We have
loved our own inside a greater environment of systematized
contempt.

And when America turned away from our Black men,
when America chose to characterize our men as animals or
rapists or shiftless or simpletons or, anyhow, and this was
always the point, anyway, *unemployable,* when America rejected our fathers and brothers and sweethearts and sons
when they came looking for work, and when America allowed big corporations like Chrysler and General Motors to
skip town because they'd discovered a labor force even
cheaper than Black men, we, Black women, kept things together, you know, not perfectly, but we did it/somebody had
to keep things together and we didn't never skip town. We

didn't never say, "I'll be back. I'm going to the store," and then just disappear. And thank God, or else, who among us, Black, male or female, would be here today? And is this what all those sophisticated types mean when they gargle out the gobbledygook about "female-headedness"?

Number Two: To continue my assessment, I would agree that the Black family is not white. I do not agree that the problem is "female-headedness." I would rather suggest that the problem is that women, in general, and that Black women, in particular, cannot raise our children and secure an adequately paying job because this is a society that hates women and that thinks we are replaceable/we are dispensable, ridiculous, irksome facts of life aptly described as "female-headed," for example. American social and economic hatred of women means that any work primarily identified as women's work will be poorly paid, if at all. Any work open to women will be poorly paid, at best, in comparison to work open to men. Any work done by women will receive a maximum of 64 cents on the dollar compared to the same work done by men. Prenatal, well-baby care, day care for children, children's allowances, housing allowances for parents of children, paid maternity leave—all of the elemental provisions for the equally entitled citizenship of women, and of children, are ordinary attributes of industrialized nations, except for one: the United States.

The problem, clearly, does not originate with women, in general, or Black women, specifically, who, whether it's hard or whether it's virtually impossible, nevertheless keep things together. Our hardships follow from the uncivilized political and economic status enjoined upon women and children in our country, which has the highest infant mortality rate among its industrial peers. And, evidently, feels fine, thank you, about that. Not incidentally, Black infant mortality rates hold at levels twice that of whites.

Number Three. The bizarre tautological analysis of the

Black family that blames the Black family for being not white/ not patriarchal not endowed with steadily employed Black husbands and fathers who enjoy access to middle-income occupations is just that: a heartless and bizarre tautology, a heartless joke. Supposing Black men and Black women *wanted* Black men to become patriarchs of their families, supposing Black men wanted to function as head of the house: shouldn't they probably have some kind of a job? And quite apart from quasi-patriarchal virtues or ambitions, shall anyone truly dare to suggest that the catastrophic 45 percent unemployment rate now crippling adult Black men is something that either Black men or Black women view as positive or desirable? Forty-five percent! What is the meaning of a man in the house if he cannot hold out his hand to help his family make it through the month, and if he cannot hold up his head with the pride and authority that regular, satisfying work for good pay provides? How or whom shall he marry and on what basis? Is it honestly puzzling to anyone that the forty-five percent Depression rate of unemployment that imprisons Black men almost exactly mirrors the forty-seven percent of Black households now headed up by Black women? Our Black families persist despite a racist arrangement of rewards such that a fully employed Black man or Black woman can hope to earn only 56 cents on the dollar as compared to the remuneration received by whites for equal work. And a Black college graduate, male or female, still cannot realistically expect to earn more than a white high school graduate.

We, children and parents of Black families, neither created nor do we control the terrible, deteriorating state of our unjust and meanly discriminating national affairs. In its structure, the traditional Black family has always reflected our particular jeopardy within these unwelcome circumstances. We have never been "standard" or predictable or stabilized in any normative sense even as our Black lives have never been standard or predictable or stabilized inside a benign, nationwide environment. We have been flexible, ingenious, and innovative or we have perished. And we have not perished. We remain and we remain different, and we have become necessarily deft at distinguishing between the negative differences—those imposed upon us—and the positive differences—those that joyously attest to our distinctive, survivalist attributes as a people.

Today, we must distinguish between responsibility and consequence. We are not responsible for the systematic under- and unemployment of Black men or women. We are not responsible for the drastically unequal rewards of employment available to women and to Black adults and teenagers. We are not responsible for racist hatred of us, and we are not responsible for American contempt for women, per se. We are not responsible for a dominant value system that quibbles over welfare benefits for children and squanders deficit billions of dollars on American pie in the sky. But we must outlive the consequences of an inhumane, disposable-life ideology. We have no choice. And because our economic system and because our political system of support for that economy really do subscribe to a disposable-life ideology whenever the conflict appears to pit profit or dominant power against the freedoms of human beings, we no longer constitute a minority inside America. Perforce we have been joined in our precarious quandary, here, by women, and children, Hispanic Americans, and Native Americans and the quickly expanding population of the aged, as well as the temporarily or permanently disabled.

At issue now is the "universal entitlement" as Ruth Sidel terms it in her important book *Women and Children Last,* of American citizens: What should American citizenship confer; what are the duties of the state in relation to the citizens it presumes to tax and to govern?

It is not the Black family in crisis but American democracy in crisis when the majority of our people oppose U.S. intervention in Central America and, nevertheless, the president proceeds to intervene, albeit in circuitous and loony-tune fashion. And the bullets and the bombs falling out from such executive overriding of democratic representation will neither amuse nor merely make believe their unconscionable destruction inside Nicaragua. It is not the Black family in crisis but American democracy at stake when the majority of our people abhor South African apartheid and, nonetheless, the president proceeds to collaborate with the leadership of that evil up to the utmost of his ability to stay awake. It is not the Black family in crisis but American democracy at risk when a majority of American citizens may no longer assume the preservation and/or the development of social programs to let them stay alive and well.

But if we, Black children and parents, have been joined in our precarious quandary, here, may we not also now actively join with these other jeopardized Americans to redefine and to finally secure universal entitlement of citizenship that will at last conclude the shameful American history of our oppression? What should these universal entitlements include?

1. Guaranteed jobs and/or guaranteed income to assure each and every American in each and every one of the fifty states an existence *above* the poverty line.

2. Higher domestic minimum wages and, for the sake of our narrow and broadest self-interests, both, a coordinated, international minimum wage so that exhausted economic exploitation in Detroit can no longer be replaced by economic exploitation in Taiwan, or Soweto, or Manila.

3. Child allowances from the state as well as state guarantees of child support.

4. Equal pay for equal work.

5. Affirmative action to assure broadly democratic access to higher-paying occupations.

6. Compensation for "women's work" equal to compensation for "men's work."

7. Housing allowances and/or state commitments to build and/or to subsidize acceptable, safe, and affordable housing for every citizen.

8. Comprehensive, national health insurance from prenatal through geriatric care.

9. State education, and perpetual reeducation, available through graduate levels of study on the basis of student interest and aptitude rather than financial capacity.

10. A national budget that will invariably commit the main portion of our collective monies to our collective domestic needs for a good life.

11. Comprehensive provision for the well-being of all of our children commensurate with the kind of future we are hoping to help to construct. These provisions must include paid maternity/paternity leave and universal, state-controlled child-care public programs for working parents.

12. Nationalization of vital industries to protect citizen consumers and citizen workers, alike, from the greed-driven vagaries of a "free market."

13. Aggressive nuclear disarmament polices and, concurrently, aggressive state protection of what's left of the life-supportive elements of our global environment.

I do not believe that a just, a civilized nation can properly regard any one of these thirteen entitlements as optional. And yet, not one of them is legally in place. And, as these rudimentary aspects of democratic entitlement exist nowhere on our American landscape today, and as Black women and Black men have been historically targeted for the worst social and economic forms of American rejection, is there any reason—any *reason*—for surprise that we may in our Black American daily attempts to keep going evince so many signs of enormous, arduous strain? Who is surprised? And why do we tolerate these expert yammerings/these insufferable accusations of Black family breakdown/Black *moral* breakdown? Black breakdown compared to what?

In the current American context that produces such stunning overall statistics as these—two out of every three officially poor Americans are women and one out of every two marriages ends in divorce—it seems to me that we, Blackfolks, are holding up rather well!

And in the current American atmosphere of moral leadership provided by Ronald Reagan, our American president who grievously breaks international and national law and then regularly lies about those crimes or, better yet, just *forgets* about them—in this atmosphere, who shall presume to say *what* to the domestic victims of this, our executive criminal? We need rescue from his crimes! We do not need the cruel absurdity of patronizing criticism precisely because our beleaguered lives expose the inhumane consequences of Ronald Reagan's complete code of national dishonor! Since his accession to the presidency, is there *any* federal program for domestic life-support that has not come under his personal, his unpardonable, attack?

And what about teenage pregnancy which, like divorce, has moved forward into critical, destabilizing areas of contemporary dynamics? I say there is nothing inherently bad about young people wanting to become mothers or fathers. There is nothing specifically Black about it, either, or white. It's happening, now, with greater frequency than the teenagers themselves, or the rest of us, can readily accommodate in a civilized, supportive, nondestructive manner. And that's because extremely few Americans apparently know how to successfully mother or father, anyway, and, also, our government is not in the habit of trying to be helpful to new parents, whether they are thirty-five years old or seventeen. As a matter of fact, American adults stutter so hypocritically about teenage pregnancies that we on the one hand claim to be upset but then we still can't get it together to guarantee appropriate, universal sex education in our public schools, and universal teenage access to contraceptive means, including abortion, if necessary. I note that, actually, teenage pregnancy rates have declined by 10 percent during the decade from 1973 to 1983. And I note that, notwithstanding that fact, the alarm continues, hysterical and, again, misbegotten in its aim. Before anybody presumes to condemn or to take away the children of our children, we need to confront these questions. Who will instinctively respect a Black boy or a young Black girl? Who needs them? Who cannot live without them? Who else will welcome, without ambivalence, the advent of another Black child besides a Black child, herself, or himself? Who among us is prepared to answer any of those questions with a dedicated programmatic evidence of sincerity? First, it seems to me, we would need to eliminate the reality of 50 percent *plus* unemployment that has taunted young Black men and women for more than ten years in America. And, second, we would need to eliminate the institutionalized educational failure that a 40 to 75 percent high school dropout rate among Black teenagers reveals. Are we ready to do that? Listen to this silence!

Compared to the uncertain, but essential, top-to-bottom, male and female, White and Black, childhood-to-elderly tough coalitional work ahead of us, the revolutionary work that will establish those thirteen universal entitlements as our new American Bill of Rights, compared to that stupendous but unavoidable, that emergency undertaking, wouldn't it be fun, instead, to duck into an old movie? You know, that old flick about the Negro Problem or is it the Crisis of the Black Family, or will it be that favorite midnight horror show about "female-headed" monstrosities that catapult an entire people into a cauldron of low-income misery and sloth? Well, go ahead, and

good luck inside the movies, and even more good luck to you
when you come out again!

In *The State of Black America, 1986*, published by the National Urban League, you will discover these rather tasty mor-
sels of new information:

In most discussions of the recent growth in female-headed families, one
fact is invariably omitted—that the largest increases occurred among
"middle class" and not "underclass" families. Nine out of every 10 (88%)
black female-headed families formed between 1970 and 1981 were headed
by women with at least a high school diploma while one out of three
were college educated. Contrary to popular belief, only 12% of the
increase in one-parent black families over this period was due to families
headed by women who were high school dropouts.

Similarly, 95% of the one-parent black families formed between 1970
and 1981 were headed by women who had been formerly married . . .
only 5% of the rise in black one-parent families during the 1970's
occurred among women who had *never* married. Similar findings result
for female-headed families among whites as well. In short, the largest
increases in one-parent families . . . occurred among the black and white
middle class—primarily because of spiraling divorce rates over the past
two decades. Thus, there is less and less empirical support for the
popular view that female-headed families are an intrinsic characteristic of
a "culture of poverty."

A couple of pages later we read,

. . . Black youth from one-parent families are about as likely to attend
college as are youth from two-parent families. While 13% of children in
two-parent families were in college in 1979, so were 10% of the children
in one-parent black families. Similarly, among black families with
incomes of $20,000 and over, youth in two-parent families were about as
likely to attend college (20%) as youth in one-parent black families
(23%).

But all of these numbers and percentile comparisons don't
do too much for ghetto culture products like myself. I mean all

that's useful. And I'm mighty glad to find out that the—what do they call that stuff? empirical data?—move right along in synch with my own head and my own heart. But I personally do not need any of these supersophisticated charts and magical graphs to tell me my own momma done better than she could and my momma's momma, *she* done better than I could. And *everybody's momma* done better than anybody had any right to expect she would. And that's the truth!

And I hope you've been able to follow my meaning. And a word to the wise, they say, should be sufficient. So, I'm asking you real nice: Don't you talk about my momma.

PARK SLOPE:
MIXING IT UP
FOR GOOD

O I see flashing that this America is only you and me . . .
Freedom, language, poems, employments, are you and me,
Past, present, future, are you and me.
I dare not shirk any part of myself. . . .

—Walt Whitman, from "By Blue Ontario's Shore"

SOUNDTRACK, THE SOPHISTICATED, BUSTLING MUSIC STORE
that Tommy Spennato opened eight years ago on Park Slope's
main drag, Seventh Avenue, confronts would-be consumers
with a dazzling catholicity of albums, CDs, and cassettes in
orderly bins and on display. From classical to reggae, from
heavy jazz to Kool and the Gang or Ethel Waters or Milton
Nascimento or UB40, it's all there because, for Spennato's
customers, it's all popular music: Park Slope is a popular,
a democratic neighborhood, as mixed-up, or as cosmopolitan,
as an inventory of Spennato's musical stock would readily
suggest.

This mix is what the thirty-eight-year-old proprietor loves.

This essay was originally published in the *New York Times* on November 20, 1988.

As he says, "I'm ethnic! I'm successful! I like the idea that I work in the neighborhood where I grew up! I like the fact of my family living here: it just makes me feel good."

At The Paper Place, Leonid Guzmán, a local stationer, speaks angrily or with sadness in his voice. His current lease, like Tommy Spennato's, expires in two years, and he worries about the landlord: will he strike out for gold? If so, Guzmán says, quietly, "I can't do it. I'm not willing to work for the landlord. I'm working for my family!"

More than a few people are worried these days in Park Slope. They worry about the threat to their Walt Whitman dream of an egalitarian urban paradise, where people live well beyond tolerance, delighting in the audiovisual differences that their various lives reveal. At least middle-class in income or the average cost of the sneakers everybody seems to wear everywhere, it is not, however, white. For example, five of about twenty brownstones on my block are owned and occupied by Black families. And, in my co-op building, you will find only two white households out of a total of four.

Around the corner, Judy Huang, a young woman recently here from China, manages the laundry and delights in practicing her beginner's Spanish. She will tease you with "¿Cómo estás?" before turning away to hunt for your particular load of washed, dried, and folded clothing. Across the street, Fuji-San, the first sushi bar in the area, thrives underneath a parlor-floor restaurant offering Mexican food. In the meantime, if you have walked just one block from my apartment up to Garfield Place you may very well have passed by a Korean produce and flower stand, a retired white blue-collar worker and his soon-to-be-retired Airedale, any number of single young white professionals, two Black pre-teenagers in identical new outfits, and Irish or Italian male "youths" idling even when it rains.

Park Slope is good because it's mixed. It explodes a slew of nasty commonplaces: that benefits of urban integration entail the sacrifice of middle-class concerns such as stable, or rising, property values, safety on the streets, and fresh vegetables; that you cannot happily juxtapose the elderly, the middle-aged, and young, unmarried men and women; that an open and busy and constant and variously "hanging out" kind of pedestrian street life is dangerous; that gentle or safe necessarily means white or affluent or monochromatic anything whatsoever.

Park Slope is good because it was designed to deliver a graceful way of life. Bounded by Flatbush Avenue to the north, Prospect Park to the east, Ninth Street to the south, and Fifth Avenue to the west, the neighborhood is crowned by Grand Army Plaza—a monumental mesh of a traffic island complete with formal garden, a lofty Civil War memorial arch, and a dizzy circling of cars, buses, and trucks. The eastern limit to Park Slope amounts to no limit at all. Prospect Park provides for grandiose escape from every kind of personal confinement. Steeply sloping down from that high green boundary, the streets abound with pristine rows of four-story limestone and brownstone houses evidently cherished since the start of the century and frequently shaded by tall trees flourishing in their generous maturity.

The scale is intimate. The look is elegant. The controlling architectonic ideas are huge and, therefore, imperturbable. In Prospect Park it doesn't matter whether Haitian soccer teams or Italian volleyball players or Rastafarian music lovers congregate. The visionary genius of Frederick Law Olmsted and Calvert Vaux, America's pioneer designers of democratic public parks, anticipated and invites exactly such mass multiple consumption of communal outside space.

The typical Park Slope brownstone may house one well-to-do family with a live-in maid lodged on the fourth floor or, more commonly now, four or five co-op or rental households. The painstaking and spacious original construction of these houses remains intact: one, two, or five families can make themselves, solidly, at home. And they do. In the remarkable urban community of Park Slope, a uniquely American amalgam of New Yorkers makes itself at home.

Park Slope as a residential neighborhood dates to the completion of Prospect Park in 1873. At that time, developers constructed a "gold coast" of mansions on the western edge of the park and then subsequently built more modest, middle-class and working-class homes. The rich lived at the top of the slope. Behind and below them, Irish and Italian immigrant families ensconced themselves.

At the conclusion of World War II, the offspring of these immigrants emigrated to the suburbs and thereby deprived the neighborhood of residents thirty to forty-four years old (the group commonly regarded as the spine of a desirable and forward-moving community). Into this vacuum, poor Black and Puerto Rican families moved during the 1950s in small but apparently significant numbers that subsequently have not declined. As newcomers, they met with hostility and white flight, and some old-timer residents came to believe that Park Slope had gone "bad." In the meantime, teenage gangs like the Italian Golden Guineas fought with each other for territory or for the hell of it.

For a decade or more, city services attenuated or disappeared. Not until the late sixties did communal image and attitude turn around once again: venturesome young white couples began to arrive, buying today's $750,000 to $900,000 Park Slope brownstones for as little as $12,000. Many of them spent the next fifteen years renovating their homes with a do-it-yourself zeal for restoration rather than change. In general, they would strip, sand, and stain-by-hand their Victorian window shutters rather than remove them.

And, just as Grand Army Plaza crowns the architectural beauty of Park Slope, and just as the 526 acres of Prospect Park suffuse the bordering environment with a physical sense of natural balance and relief, the Celebrate Brooklyn Performing Arts Festival promotes the rich cultural meaning of America per se and of Park Slope in particular. Now in its tenth year, the Celebrate Brooklyn series was invented by Burl Hash, a long-term resident of Park Slope. On any summer night, you can stand or dance or sit or lie down under the stars and enjoy the live performances of artists as varied as the vocal group Sweet Honey in the Rock, or the Brooklyn Philharmonic Orchestra, or the gifted young American composer and keyboard artist Adrienne Torf and her band. In variety and magical vigor, the audience and the artists seem well-met indeed.

Local benefit dinners for Celebrate Brooklyn may be catered by the New Prospect Café, which its proprietors call a sweaty neighborhood restaurant, just north of Grand Army Plaza on Flatbush Avenue. The three relatively young owners of this casual place regularly contribute their catering skills and edibles, at cost, on behalf of political and cultural undertakings as diverse as the Brooklyn Academy of Music and the Gay Men's Health Crisis.

Last year, for their third anniversary party, Michael Gross, Stacey Cretakos, and John Guimby, the partnership behind New Prospect Café, threw a gigantic community party to which they invited their regular Park Slope customers. Pure Excitement, a Park Slope pop and reggae band, provided the entertainment. Headed by the lead vocalist, Sonia Smith, Pure Excitement features her husband, Karel Smith, on drums. For more than twenty years, he has been the resident shoemaker of Park Slope, operating out of a humble Seventh Avenue storefront between Lincoln Place and St. John's. In June 1988, Smith's landlord appeared in the doorway of the little shop and announced a monthly rent hike from $700 to $2,300, effective immediately.

I am sitting on a bench on Union Street across from the Port Royal Club, a local nightspot where the New Prospect Café held its annual party. The club's owner is a Black man, fifty-three-year-old Harold Dixon, who, like Karel Smith, came from Jamaica two decades ago and settled his family in Park Slope. In contrast to Mr. Smith, Mr. Dixon owns his Park Slope bicycle shop, the building that houses it, and the Port Royal Club besides.

The two men have been talking energetically for a while when I join their animated company. Visceral panic clouds Karel Smith's eyes. "How does it feel to put another man's family on the street?" He shakes his head, incredulous. "The man him have no mercy!"

Harold Dixon leaps to his feet, a lithe and wiry athlete, enraged by the prospects that face his friend: "You tell him him must get out! Get out! And go to court! There can't be no judge in the world that will say a man him fix up shoes can pay out $2,300 a month—a shoemaker man! Aaagh!" He jolts back to the bench. "It's greed!"

Money hunger could destroy the life of Karel Smith. Greed could wreck Park Slope, demolish its democracy, homogenize the population, evict many of these striving, quiet people from their homes, and erase the community-spawned services that still characterize most of the small businesses on Seventh Avenue. It's happening now.

Some would say it's been happening. Michael Gross reports a terrible rise in the number of going-away parties at New Prospect Café. "Some people got really hacked off about the rents, and they've gone off to Indiana or Seattle or Vermont."

The wonder is that none of the predictable card tables set up on Saturdays outside the Key Food supermarket on Seventh Avenue and offering petitions for signatures on issues ranging from nonintervention in Central America to nuclear missiles berthed in Brooklyn harbors—the wonder is that none of the political petitions ever focuses on the need for residential and commercial rent stabilization.

Park Slope is not politically naïve, or unimportant. When Nicaragua's president, Daniel Ortega Saavedra, made a diplomatic trip to the United States in 1986, he stopped at the Park Slope Methodist Church as well as at the United Nations. That church, boasting the most activist congregation of the ten churches and one synagogue clustered inside the neighborhood, had regularly held benefit poetry readings and sponsored worker brigade delegations to Nicaragua. And last spring, during an exhausting primary campaign in which the Reverend Jesse Jackson could not always appear where he was expected, he did not fail to address the Park Slope rally in front of P.S. 321.

In fact, in its vitality and public social ease, Park Slope's way of life echoes the more democratic attributes of Cambridge, Massachusetts, or Berkeley, California. The difference is that, here, our university is urban life itself.

It's a cool bright morning in Park Slope. It's time to ride. From 10 A.M. to 3 P.M., Prospect Park becomes a safe preserve for cyclists, runners, and other more pedestrian aficionados of the trees and grass. I am pushing my twelve-speed Peugeot out to the stoop. Below the front stairs and over by the garbage cans is Ruth Smith, a Black woman probably younger than I am. She is homeless. I thought she had died, last winter, when I no longer saw her sleeping under newspapers, on the granite steps of the Seventh Avenue Dutch Reformed Church across from Tommy Spennato's Soundtrack. She has not died. She has found two empty Canada Dry Seltzer bottles. She adds these to the pile of empties that fills her shopping cart. "Good morning, Mrs. Smith," I call. Now she looks at me, remembers, and, at last, returns a somberly spoken "Good morning, June."

I am on my way to a seven-mile ride around the park. I can almost feel the coming thrill of downhill flight by bike. Where will she go next? What will she find that is beautiful? Why does she stay in Park Slope? "I am a healer," she told me, once. "I keep everybody alive in this community." I had asked her, how did she do that? "I keep everybody alive with a look or a touch, or by prayer."

I am not inclined to doubt the truth of this. We see Ruth Smith. She lives among us. She wishes us well. She asks very little, evidently oblivious to her own endangered existence. And we would be foolish to ignore the parable of her continuing life in our community. We would be crazy to assume her survival, or our own.

FINDING THE HAYSTACK IN THE NEEDLE, OR, THE WHOLE WORLD OF AMERICA AND THE CHALLENGE OF HIGHER EDUCATION

THAT OLD ADAGE ABOUT FINDING A NEEDLE IN THE HAYSTACK has always troubled me. Why would you do that to a needle in the first place? Or, if you happened to lose it, why wouldn't you try to find something else, something more likely, and useful, in that situation of stacked-up hay? And what about that hay? How come nobody's out looking for that common, big messy thing: that food, that playground that children and lovers enjoy?

Do we believe—we who live upon the 3,675,547 square miles of the continental United States land mass—do we really believe that "big," or that "big and various," does not matter? i.e., that "big and various" cannot be ruined or lost?

By definition, and by contrast, a good needle is something small, something narrow and, by itself, utterly useless. It does not grow anywhere. It cannot be eaten. Junkies use it. And, also, a camel can more easily pass through its eye than a rich man can enter the Kingdom of Heaven. As a matter of fact, the very idea of a needle is that of a difficult trick: it's a barrier you have to get into in order to get out of—in order to get over. No one will ever undertake to thread a needle with her eyes closed or one hand tied behind her back or without thinking about it to the point of excruciating expectation of failure.

Until quite recently, American education has venerated the needle and scorned the unruly, combustible, and gigantic haystack of our increasingly heterogeneous population. Higher education has meant higher than most of the people. The best universities have continued the worst kind of class privilege. They have enshrined tyrannical reflections of Western white male narcissism. These blinding needles, these (trying-to-look-like) ivory towers, have erected themselves stiff and imperturbable above the multimillionfold folk realities of everyday suffering and rage. They even celebrate the height of their distance from such mass disturbances as homelessness and battered wives. Instead, they commit themselves to an exorbitant and sometimes fatal mythology of "pure research" and/or "pure science."

Thus we have nuclear missiles and chemical defoliants but we do not have clean rivers or a cure for AIDS. Thus we have a surfeit of information about the daydreams of eighteenth-century lords and their ladyfriends, but we do not know the meaning of Monday morning to an unmarried teenage mother or a middle-aged Navajo father who cannot find a reason to stop drinking himself to death.

Until quite recently, the regular rule of thumb for measuring excellence in higher education was pretty crude stuff indeed: the smaller the eye of the needle, the better the school. The more people your standards of admission could reject, the more people and cultures and histories and spoken languages other than your own that you could exclude from your core curriculum—or patronize—the better the school.

The best higher education available in the U.S.A. has meant that you could graduate *summa cum laude* certainly knowing about the fictive tragedy of King Lear, but absolutely ignorant about the actual prayers, the chants, the dances, the burial mounds, and the deeply reverent and unifying perspectives of Native Americans. You would definitely memorize the dates of major Anglo-Saxon battles, but you would remain unable to name or explain a single Chinese dynasty. You would never ever split an infinitive or end a sentence with a preposition, but you could not understand why other people—for example African-Americans and Puerto Ricans and Amerasians and Vietnamese and Japanese and Lebanese and Senegalese and Chinese and Chicanos and Pakistanis seemed so stubbornly dependent upon and even rooted to their own "weird" mother tongue.

Why couldn't they learn to speak or write "plain English"? You could work your way, Phi Beta Kappa, through one of the super-superfine needles of our country and, nevertheless, believe that Sandino is the Spanish word for Marx.

This was a comfortable status quo for a powerful few. But there exist, evidently, some serious contradictions between the aims of a dominant world power and a ruling elite that knows little or nothing about the people it chooses to ignore and/or colonize and/or exterminate. That disjuncture between would-be power and knowledge has toppled these United States into second- and third-rate jeopardies on international as well as domestic levels.

We have become a colossal world nation ill-equipped for worldwide competition in the invention, production, and export of goods and technologies that the species will cherish or demand. Our arrogant disregard of revolutionary need on earth has placed us, repeatedly, on the side of brute suppression of human outcries for rescue and relief. An embarrassing number of young Americans cannot accurately describe the geographic differences between Mexico and New Jersey—let alone the difference between Tanzania and Nigeria.

Our official display of needle mentality means that nobody is home at the White House when the Kremlin calls off the Cold War. Or our gentler and kinder leading light will presume to say he "approves" of the democratic changes taking place in some entirely other country—for instance, the sovereign state of the Polish people, who by the way are not native speakers or writers of the English language. Or we will overtly choose to infuse the equivalent of more than two billion dollars into the criminal rigging of Nicaraguan elections where, alas, English is also a second language, if that, for most of the citizens of that beleaguered neighbor—to the north, is it? Or to the south? (And, did I say, "criminal"? Well, yes, it happens to be against international law to mine the harbors of somebody else's turf and, yes, it is also a violation of international law to meddle in the internal politics of somebody else's nation-state —whether you like their politics or not!)

And because the needlepoint intelligence at the helm of our destiny today is so lost, so confounded, and so willfully out of place inside the haystack dilemmas of the planet, the United States was, recently, one of the only two allegedly major powers to vote against the immediate banning of products that are tearing apart the protective sky above every single one of us.

It is not only hard to find a needle in a haystack; it is a misbegotten, stupid, and inhumane undertaking from the get-go. But we will have to gird ourselves for an arduous overthrow of American fantasies if we will reverse the values that now imperil our powers of self-preservation, equitable reform, and moral authority. We will have to turn away from that long-ago legendary table where our legendary Founding Fathers sat, comfortably musing about all men having been created equal while most of them maintained other human beings, African women and men and children, in slavery, and while the needling eloquence of their pioneer deliberations did not permit them to perceive the absurdity of an avowedly democratic state in which most of the subjects—all women, per se, and all white men who neither owned property nor knew how to read or write—would be automatically denied the political control that voting confers. We will have to turn from that long-ago peculiar and hallowed scenario and check out that consummate, still-standing, emblematic needle on the landscape of the U.S.A.: what do you suppose anybody had in mind when he, so to speak, conceived of the Washington Monument? And those warning red eyes at the top of it: what do they see? What do they mean besides *beware* and *stay away* and *danger*? What do they illuminate in the nighttime terror of urban America? And does that preeminent American needle point to us, the people, or to an indifferent stratosphere?

But despite the failings of the Fathers and with complete and reciprocal disregard for the Washington Monument, we are here inside the big and messy and combustible haystack of these United States, and the forecast is not good. Corporate management complains that the upcoming American labor force will prove itself illiterate and irrelevant to the tasks of the Twenty-first century. A spokesman for the current administration has publicly "acknowledged" that federal antidrug policies and commitments in effect will "write off a generation." And, incidentally, we the people did not storm and liberate the White House behind such an extraordinarily blithe and genocidal utterance. And isn't it time, perhaps, that the symbolism carried by that name, the White House—isn't it time, perhaps, that we come up with something a bit less blatant, a touch less needlelike and, wrongly, exclusive?

At home, the forecast is disquieting, at least. Some of us have looked into a future and we have seen that the future will not be white, or spoken or written in Standard English. Of course these facts imply that, finally, our domestic demographics and our domestic multihinged realities will soon become more of a microcosmic, accurate reflection of the global village just outside our national boundaries.

Is this good news or bad?

Nationwide, the fastest-growing segment of the American population speaks Spanish and, currently, it suffers from three times the high-school dropout rate for white students and two times the dropout rate for Black. Should we impose Standard English on these citizens of the U.S.A., or should we relegate the national Latino community to substandard America?

According to the *New York Times*, the state of California, "with 4.6 million students, is the nation's largest market for textbooks." A week ago, the American needlebrain lobby, calling itself the Traditional Values Coalition, won a great victory for power without knowledge. This coalition of needleheads has successfully prevailed upon the California school board to retreat from what the coalition has characterized as "an overemphasis on the theory of evolution." Consequently, the board has deleted two sentences from its guidelines for textbooks dealing with the origin and development of life on earth, to wit:

1. "There is no scientific dispute that evolution has occurred and continues to occur; this is why evolution is regarded as a scientific fact."

2. "These sequences show that life has continually diversified through time, as older species have been replaced by newer ones."

The questions underlying the haystack and the needles are these: How will Americans and how will American education confront the evolution of the American people into a more and

more diversified citizenry that will require the democratic replacement of currently powerful interests with new ones?

Will we knuckle under to the needleheads? Will we simply
delete vast American communities from our national vision?
Will we persist in our eagerness to spend in excess of twenty
thousand dollars per prisoner, per year, for the imprisonment
of a disproportionate number of Black men while we begrudge
the inadequate pittance of state monies allocated, yearly, to
our community colleges where a disproportionate number of
Black and other minority students attempt to empower themselves? Will we notice that the fastest-growing segment of our
matriculated college population is Asian and yet persist in
relegating Asian history and Asian literature to the possibility
of an elective, optional, one-semester course of study pursued
within that makeshift, academic-closet insult entitled Ethnic
Studies? "Ethnic Studies"! When the Asians and the Africans
and the Indians and the Hispanic peoples of the earth constitute the majority of the human beings in the world, what kind
of higher education will not have the history and the literature
and the languages of these peoples at the absolute center of its
required curriculum? Is it, perhaps, a higher education that
has, as its purpose, as its point, the indifferent stratosphere and
not our human lives?

But never mind about the haystack of the world beyond our
boundaries. According to the California Commission for the
Review of the Master Plan for Higher Education, 1987:

> In the year 2000, it is estimated that whites will comprise only 53.6%,
> with Hispanics at 26.8%, Asians and others at 11.8%, and Blacks at
> 7.9% of the state's population. Sometime between 2000 and 2010,
> non-Hispanic whites will no longer constitute a majority, making
> California the first mainland state without a majority racial group.

Is this good news or bad?

If the fate of a country depends upon the well-being and

knowledge of its citizens, and if America perseveres in its peculiar veneration of the needle, then we're in trouble.

At the moment, 80 percent of all California freshmen are sitting in second- and third-rate classrooms of one or another community college. But to understand these statistics you need an overall picture of statewide education politics. The public system of higher education in California divides into three tiers, as follows:

There are 1,277,900 American students in California state community colleges.

There are 355,166 American students in the state of California universities.

And there are 161,522 American students on the University of California campuses.

Per student, per year, the state spends $2,899 on the community college level, $6,617 on the California state university level, and $13,260 per student, per year, on the University of California level.

What's the operating principle here? "To them that have it will be given"? "From those that have not it will be taken away"?

As Carl Friedlander, an English teacher at Los Angeles Community College, writes in a letter bristling with egalitarian indignation, "Clearly, the students who need the most get the least."

And, because only 4.5 percent of all Black high school graduates even qualify for admission to the University of California, and because only 5 percent of all Latino high school graduates qualify, the California state-starved community college is the overwhelming single opportunity for higher education accessible to minority Americans.

I visited that Los Angeles Community College ten days ago.

An estimated one thousand students voluntarily chose to pack two auditoriums plus an additional lobby area in order to hear what was billed as a poetry reading. As the poet of the occasion, I felt entirely intimidated: there must be some mistake! Perhaps a movie had been scheduled for the same place and time, and I was the mistake?

Feeling the full-throttle energy of that young and utterly various throng of Chinese and Chicano and African-American and Salvadoran students, I panicked and told my host, "I'm outahere!" Thinking about the poems I had written—most of them in Standard English and not enough of them in Black English and absolutely none of them in Spanish or in any other language—I felt completely inadequate and ill-prepared. But my host firmly seized me by my shoulders and would not let me go. And so I struggled to present these young Americans with the necessarily limited truth my poetry can convey. As the minutes went by, I found myself less and less inclined to try and reach outside my most intimate universe by choosing poems about Nicaragua or Guatemala or Palestine. Instead, my instincts led me to settle upon the poetry that I have written in my given language: the language of my home—Black English. And, to my incredible surprise and delight, the students of that gathering embraced this language and did not reject its specificity or its frame of reference—which is, in fact, the idiosyncratic truth of my personal experience. And I loved them for their generosity. And, afterwards, during the question-and-answer session that ensued, we talked about that, together, the audience and I. We talked about language and poetry and the politics of telling the truth in relation to language and poetry and how I felt grateful to them for their generous reception of my poems and now I understood from seeing them and from coming among them that I must attempt a further diversification and expansion of the languages my poetry will employ and how I must attempt new poems that will better deserve the gentle willingness of their intelligent attention.

And following upon this mass interchange, some of the faculty and staff of Los Angeles Community College met with me and I learned these facts about their institution:

• There is no campus nurse or health faculty, of any kind.
• There is no psychological counseling program.
• There is no job-placement center.
• There is no football team.
• Programs in nursing, optics, dental assistance, occupational therapy, and radiologic technology have been eliminated.
• There is no women's center.
• There is no African-American studies program or department.
• There is no ethnic studies program or department.
• There are no doors on the bathroom stalls.
• Composition classes and English as a Second Language classes have 40 students each; the typical composition teacher teaches 150 students every semester, and two-thirds of these are students whose native language is not English.

Let me repeat this:

The typical composition teacher teaches five classes of 30 students each, or 150 students every semester, and two-thirds of these students are Americans whose native language is not English.

I listened to this appalling list of state crimes against the people and before I could stop myself I blurted out, "Let them come and talk canon to these students!" These needlekeepers of "the canon" who travel, coast to coast, on the attack against the scientific fact of evolution, the political significance of quantum mechanics, the social and political and educational requirements of heterogeneous America, the fading credibility

98

of seventeenth-century Restoration drama in England, or our slowly developing knowledge of *Native Son* or *Coming of Age* (Black) *in Mississippi* or Native American *Ceremonies* or *The Beans of Egypt, Maine* or *Joy Luck Club* wisdom and woe or *Obasan* models of cultural lineage, or Adrienne Rich explorations of contemporary forms and quandaries of moral conscience, or Angela Davis examples of defiance and triumph.

And I thought, "Let the needlekeepers of the canon come to this community college and, first thing, put doors on the bathroom stalls, and then raise enough money for one nurse who can answer emergency health calls arising from this total student body of 15,000 young Americans! And otherwise, let them just sit around the Washington Monument and, worshipping the past and the dead, let them eventually levitate to that eerie, pure level of those warning red eyes, and then let them continue, elevating themselves away from the people we are, until they disintegrate, ecstatic, in some completely rarefied stratum of the indifferent stratosphere."

But, by all means, keep them out of the classrooms of these United States. Danger! Beware the needleheads! We have a combustible haystack of problems to study and sort and solve. A 4.5 percent university eligibility rate of high school achievement for Black students means what, explicitly, about the 95.5 percent majority who do not qualify?

What does it mean about our high schools that compel their daily attendance?

A 5 percent university eligibility rate of high school achievement for Latino students means what, explicitly, about the 95 percent majority who do not qualify?

What does it mean about the competitive and peaceable future of these United States?

And what do these statistics imply about the viability of a canon of human literature that was carefully constructed in the image of a white man, now deceased, who once wrote whatever he had to say in a country we waged a revolution to become independent of?

And if the savagely antidemocratic deficiencies of public commitment to our community colleges will not yield to conventional political protest, then shouldn't we take it to the courts?

If this national disgrace does not qualify as a profound provocation for a class-action suit against the crimes of the state against the people, then what will?

The challenge of higher education in the whole world of America is this: to lift the standards of the teachers and of the required core curriculum so that we who would teach can look into the eyes of those who would learn from us without shame and without the perversions of ignorance disguised as Noble Mystery.

And for those of us stranded inside the conundrum of teaching English to a fully entitled American population that is neither English nor, increasingly, born to the language of those who set the standards for power in our country, perhaps we can try to teach what we are learning, now, with so much pain and with so much eager but timorous hope: If you want to talk with somebody you have to arrive at the same language, somehow. And/but talking the same language cannot and must not mean "my language and not yours" or "your language and not mine." It means finding a way to understand, not to change or to eclipse or to obliterate but to understand each other.

And there are many languages. There is the language of guns. There is the language of money. There is the language of human rights. There is the language of mercy. There is the language of love.

And is it not marvelous and is it not true that we *can* learn to speak and read and write a language that will preserve and expand and deepen and not destroy our evolving human consciousness?

And is it not amazing that an Indian, a Native American poet of our country and in our time, has taken herself into the Navajo landscape that we may call the Arizona desert and there she has written down these words for us:

I can hear the sizzle of newborn stars, and know anything of meaning, of fierce magic, emerging here. I am witness to flexible eternity, the evolving past, and I know we will live forever, as dust or breath in the face of stars, in the shifting pattern of winds.[1]

[1]Joy Harjo and Stephen Strom, *Secrets from the Center of the World* (Tucson: University of Arizona Press, 1989).

THE MOUNTAIN
AND THE MAN WHO
WAS NOT GOD

An Essay on the Life

and Ideas of

Dr. Martin Luther King, Jr.

BIOGRAPHY
David J. Garrow
"Bearing the Cross: Martin Luther King Jr. and the
Southern Christian Leadership Conference"

Mr. Garrow, a 33-year-old associate professor of political science at City
College and the Graduate Center of the City University of New York, won
for his biography of the slain civil-rights leader. Mr. Garrow was born in
New Bedford, Mass., graduated from Wesleyan University in 1975 and
earned master's and doctoral degrees from Duke University. His biography
of the Rev. Dr. Martin Luther King Jr. detailed his inner torment over his
sexual adventuring and the Federal Bureau of Investigation's attempts to use
this weakness to destroy him.

—Announcement of Pulitzer Prize, *New York Times,* April 17, 1987

This was an address delivered at Stanford University on January 20, 1987. It was
published in June Jordan, *Moving Towards Home: Selected Political Essays* (London:
Virago Press, 1989).

ANYTIME YOU DECIDE TO TAKE ON A MOUNTAIN YOU JUST BET-
ter take good care. It's not about running out of the house. It's
not about come as you are. It's not about breaking down that
mighty, miraculous fact of the earth into little pieces or clumps
of dirt that you feel you can comfortably deal with. Anytime
you decide to take on a mountain, the irreducible is that you're
taking on something mysterious, something huge, something
more enormous than you can ever hope to hold between your
hands or even between your ears. First and last, the point is the
mountain as a mountain. And you would be well advised to
ascertain the indisputable height and the full, the awesome
girth of that great rising-up before you begin your serious
approach. You would be well advised to notice the invitation
of its physical entirety to the sun, the complexity of the flowers
and the foliage at its base, the frozen purity of the snow that
tops its pinnacle. You would be foolish not to calculate the
absolute difference between your own small stature, your own
limiting frailties, and the implacable, the humbling dimensions
of the mountain before you make a move.

Martin Luther King, Jr., was not a god, but he was certainly
a man of God. He was not a saint, yet he lives on, miraculous:
a mountain of a life. And perhaps some people seeking to
understand the meaning of Dr. King, perhaps some of them
forget that he was not a god, because he longed so deeply and
he labored so hard to be good, to be a good man.

If you have never seen a mountain, you may perilously fail
to recognize it even as you stand inside its shadow, or climb
into its light. If you have never known a man certain of his
faults, doubtful of his merits, *and* longing and laboring to be
good, you may mistake him for a hypocrite, or worse. But that
will mean you never understood; you never grasped the ground
rules for a fruitful, striving life. The goal is perfection, but the
one who reaches high is, by definition, someplace not exalted

and someone quite imperfect: fortunately for this earth of ours, the faithful, striving man must be a very human being.

And there are other reasons why any one of us might fail to recognize a mountain or somebody trying "to feed the hungry," trying "to clothe those who were naked," trying "to love and serve humanity"; trying to be a good man. On a worldwide landscape mutilated by games of arrogance and domination how should we come to know the name of any man except the man who makes money, or the man who makes of someone else a loser, or the man who can make somebody else cower and die? In the twentieth century, except perhaps for Mahatma Gandhi, who could stand beside Martin Luther King, Jr., and say to the believing multitudes, "I have a dream"? In the history of these United States, who shall sit in front of Dr. King saying, "I despair but I will not give up: I continue to believe in our collective capacity to love justice more than the smiling ease of compromise or the glittering profits of unearned privilege. I continue to believe in our collective capacity to test non-violence as the alternative to species' annihilation."

And today in our country, where a Black man can be lynched like twenty-three-year-old Timothy Lee in Concord, California, fourteen months ago, or beaten and chased and murdered like twenty-three-year-old Michael Griffith in Howard Beach, New York, or tomorrow afternoon in Cairo, Illinois, or next week in Amherst, Massachusetts, today, in our country, where any Black man can be randomly set upon by other Americans as they yell, "There's a bunch of niggers in the pizza parlor. Let's go kill them!"—how should anyone recognize a Black man of God, a Black man trying to redeem all of America from what he perceived to be "the evils" of racism, militarism, and capitalism? He was an anomaly: a mountain on the desert of our time.

How should we know and respect and honor his name? Or why should we bother? He was not a god. Dr. King did not invent Montgomery, Alabama, or the Women's Political Caucus of Montgomery, or Mrs. Rosa Parks. Dr. King did not invent the political independence of the Black Church in America, or the irresistible charisma of Black Baptist oratory. Dr. King did not invent the obdurate hatred and stupidity of Bull Connor or the neo-Nazis of Cicero, or, for that matter, the meticulous web of strangulating segregation in which he himself was born.

He made big mistakes. He was not a wonderful administrator. He did not abstain from whiskey, tobacco, or sex. He was not a fabulous husband, or father. He committed adultery. His apparent attitude towards women was conventional, at best, or strikingly narrow, or mean. He loved to party: dancing, horsing around, heavyweight southern cuisine, and pretty women. He did like him a little sugar in his bowl.

He was not a god.

And I remember listening to WBAI-FM radio in 1963 the way my parents long ago used to listen to AM radio broadcasts of the Joe Louis fights, only I was following the evolution of the Civil Rights Revolution: I was following the liberation of my life according to the Very Reverend Dr. King. And when, one afternoon, that fast-talking, panic-stricken newscaster in Birmingham reported the lunging killer police dogs and the atrocious hose water and I could hear my people screaming while the newscaster shouted out the story of my people, there, in Birmingham, who would not quit the streets—when he described how none of that horror of nightsticks or torrential water pressure or mad dogs on the attack could stop the children of Birmingham from coming out again and again to suffer whatever they must for freedom, I remember the positively stunned sensation that engulfed me: I knew that we were

winning; I knew that we would win. And before those demonstrations and underneath the melee and after the bleeding and
the lockups and the singing and the prayers, there was this
magical calm voice leading us, unarmed, into the violence of
White America. And that voice was not the voice of God. But
did it not seem to be the very voice of righteousness? That
voice was not the voice of God. But does it not, even now,
amazingly penetrate/reverberate/illuminate: a sound, a sum-
moning, somehow divine? That was the voice of a Black man
who had himself been clubbed and stabbed and shoved and
shot at and jailed and spat upon and who, repeatedly and
repeatedly and repeatedly, dared the utmost power of racist
violence to silence him. That was the voice of a leader who did
not tell others to do what he would or could not do: bodily he
gave witness to his faith that the righteous cause of his activity
would constitute his safety. Or, if not, his imminently possible
death would simply advance that righteous cause. And even
then and even there when I listened to that voice, I heard him
saying, "If any blood will flow in the streets of Birmingham let
it be our blood and not the blood of our white brothers," and
then and there he lost me. Dr. King could not persuade me
to adopt a posture that I felt was ignominious, abject, and
suicidal.

He was not a god.

And, according to his terms, I was not even trying to be
good.

Nevertheless, and five years later, when I heard the news of
Dr. King's assassination I knew that I had lost my leader: he
could not take *me* where I did not wish to go but he had taken
himself into the valley of death for my sake and he had *earned*
his way to the uncontested mountaintop as the moral spokesman for all of the powerless and despised and impoverished.
I might not agree with his tactics. But how could anyone
quarrel with the monumental evidence of his colossal courage?

I might not comprehend the relentlessly expanding context of his passionate concerns. I might resist the international, the multiracial thrust of his vision. But how should anyone accuse Dr. King of insincerity, of cynicism, or trivial or selfish motivation?

Beginning with desegregation and voting rights for Black Americans in the South, did he not develop a deep desire for justice as the fundament of every human life? Beginning with the bus boycott of Alabama, did he not develop a supremely rational, and inspired, sensitivity to the want of human rights around the world?

Almost twenty years ago, Dr. King, standing alone, publicly demanded that England and the United States both act to isolate South Africa through unequivocal severing of financial or any other connection with that heinous regime. In that same year, Dr. King stood forth, opposed to the war in Vietnam, and thereby suffered the calumny and castigation of his erstwhile peers as well as the hysterical censure of his outright foes. Evaluating America as "the greatest purveyor of violence in our time," in 1967 Dr. King, with a breadth of determination and rectitude unimaginable even now, undertook the launching of a revolution aimed against that violence, a revolution pitted against America's inequities, a revolution riveted against an American poverty of the spirit that allowed us to uproot, and decimate, a host of strangers while denying basic necessities to the homeless here at home.

He was not a god.

But was he not a prophet and a revolutionary calling for class war against an economic system consecrated to material wealth, a system responding only to grim promptings of brute greed and profit? When that devil's bullet lodged itself inside the body of Dr. Martin Luther King, he had already begun an astonishing mobilization of poor, Black, white, Latino Americans who had nothing to lose. They would challenge our government to eliminate exploitative, merciless, and war-mongering policies nationwide, or else "tie up the country" through "means of civil disobedience." Dr. King intended to organize those legions into "coercive direct actions" that would make of Babylon a dysfunctional behemoth begging for relief.

Is it any wonder he was killed?

He was not a god.

And so, when the news came April 4, 1968, that Dr. King was dead, I thought, I felt, along with millions and millions of other Black Americans, that so was love and so was all good-will and so was the soul of these United States. In fact, I wrote these words at the Atlanta funeral for Dr. King, words that I could scarcely see to write because my heart was terrified and grieving and because my eyes were full with tears:

I trust you will remember how we tried to love
above the pocket deadly need to please
and how so many of us died there
on our knees

We have lived two decades since the assassination of Dr. King. Perhaps we may now dare to assess the legacy of that mountain of a life. On a most profound level, it beckons as the legacy of a man who believed it possible to influence the speed and the substance of social change. American history devolving from his years of leadership unarguably supports this faith.

In thirteen years, at least these seismic changes occurred:

• The Civil Rights Act of 1957,
which mainly verified federal accessibility to organized pressures for the securement of civil rights.
• The Interstate Commerce Commission Act in 1961,
which desegregated interstate travel facilities.

• The Civil Rights Act of 1964,
which desegregated public accommodations and which out-
lawed racial discrimination in business and labor unions and
which legally committed the federal government to the principles of equal employment opportunity.

• The Voting Rights Bill of 1965,
which legally committed the federal government to protect
and provide for voting rights of Black Americans.

• And, in late April 1968, an Open Housing Act.

Dr. King was not a god.
He did not singlehandedly produce these cataclysmic documents or the indomitable movements that compelled their cre-
ation.

But can anyone imagine those years (from 1955 to 1968)
without Dr. King as the believing, the unquestionable, promul-
gating center of such righteous toil and tumult?

Was he not, everlastingly, articulate and resolute in searching out the grievances/the just demands that underlay ongoing
protest and revolt?

And, equally important, these movements and Dr. King
conferred "a sense of dignity and destiny" upon Black life.
Three years after his murder I stopped in the hunger county
town of Marks, Mississippi. My feet shifted uneasily in mud as
a young Black woman pointed nowhere in particular.

"This," she whispered, "this is where Dr. Martin Luther
King knelt down and cried."

I looked about me. Marks was no "beloved community."
Marks, Mississippi, revealed the truth of merciless America:
this bare dirt that would yield neither food nor shelter to the
families stranded there.

Dr. King was not a god. He could not survive that devil's
bullet, but Marks, Mississippi, survives his death, and 40 percent unemployment among young Black people—40 percent

unemployment—that provocation, that disgrace persists. And the murdering contempt for Black life continues. And so does our national need to unite in revolutionary coalitions to secure the justice that beloved community implies. And so does our need to forcibly transmute American imperialism into a willing moral power opposed to economic and political tyranny throughout the world.

And so do we: we continue, alive.

We are not gods.

But we are many.

And if we should finally adopt and carry forward the aggressively radical precepts and perceptions of Dr. King, then we will have to coalesce ourselves into a revolutionary movement; the interrelated nature of our international identity demands no less. And I would hope that we would not again impose the multiplicity of our best and desperate hopes upon the miracle of one man trying to do good.

He was not God.

And yet, behold the legacy of one man trying to do good!

We are not gods.

And we are many.

I would hope that we shall once again begin to build beloved community *not* looking for a leader but determined to respect and activate the leadership capacities within each one of us. And as we, millions of leaders of our own lives, unite according to shared values and priorities, if we are lucky enough to discover another Dr. King among us, so much the better for our good speed towards our goals. But, if we do not, then we will not languish, mute and immobilized.

We are not gods.

But we *are* many.

We shall likely differ on the means appropriate to the Third American Revolution. And if we mobilize for guaranteed jobs or guaranteed income, if we creatively antagonize for a radical, an equitable redistribution of the national wealth, then we *will* be vulnerable to an all-out savagery of repression. If we *will* resurrect Dr. King's impending call for guaranteed jobs, guaranteed income, and total disruption rather than protest, *and* if we will lift again his impending call for the nationalization of vital industries, then we *will* be subject to the ferocity of powerful resistance that revolution will always provoke.

And how, then, shall we proceed?

I would hope that tactical disputes among us will not damage or obscure strategic unity. For example, I believe it is my prerogative to struggle exclusively through nonviolent channels for change, if that is my personal choice. But I do not believe I have the right to censure a different choice made by my brothers and sisters in South Africa, or in Latin America, where they must certainly contend with a violence of evil and an evil as violent as the bullet that silenced Dr. King.

And I also believe that we have never yet pushed as mightily as we must for revolutionary change through nonviolent means.

And it seems self-evident that self-defense is basic to self-preservation.

But I do also believe that Dr. King's unending opposition to armed struggle, here, bespoke his genuine abhorrence of war as well as an unassailably rational analysis. Contrary to India, and contrary to South Africa, the untouchables, the oppressed peoples of these United States amount, at most, to a pitiful target minority of the total population.

And, apart from strategy and tactics, the motivating spirit of our political engagement will determine our success, as much as anything. The faithful striving life of Dr. King powerfully testifies to the pivotal function of belief. It truly matters. Dr. King really believed that the original, worthy impulse for this democratic state was just that, democratic. He really believed that the federal government exists to serve the people, not the other way around. He really believed that we could make allies of some of our enemies and that we must seek to do that. He really meant it when he declared he was not seeking victories for Black over white, or poor over rich; he was risking his life for justice, per se. He meant it when he said, "Justice is indivisible." *And he really expected justice to prevail.*

He was not a god. But he was a man of God. He was a Christian. And while he surely knew anger, and while he surely suffered from despair, he surely also knew the Scripture that reads,

> You shall love the Lord your God with all your heart, and with all your soul, and with all your mind. This is the great and first commandment. And a second is like it, You shall love your neighbor as yourself.
>
> Matthew 22:37–39

And I believe that the moral authority, and the astounding persuasion of Dr. King's moral appeal to the conscience of his compatriots, derived emphatically from his insistence upon love, and not hatred, as the governing energy for his always multiple assaults upon merciless inequity.

In Dr. King's spectacular, brief time among us you could find the beautiful evidence of his valor whenever and wherever you found him literally unarmed and naked to the unbridled state or kook violence of America.

You found the beautiful evidence of his colossal courage wherever and whenever he spoke aloud on behalf of convictions that isolated him among his bitterly competing and complaining peers, or wherever he spoke aloud for the sake of those who could not protect or defend him, those who could not contribute a dollar to the resources he strove so dauntlessly to gather and to share.

And I believe that in our own great moment, our current challenge of responsibility, there remain pariahs and pariah issues that we who wish to emulate that mountain of a life must claim as our own family, our own desegregated moral concerns.

I speak of the homeless in America and on the planet. I speak of African-Americans who still may not assume mortal safety of person or passage anywhere throughout the fifty states. I speak of the increasingly tenuous civil rights of the gay community threatened by quarantine and similarly virulent mentalities. I speak of the citizens of Nicaragua who cannot even rebuild their blasted homes because the United States persists in its contra-revolutionary aggressions against their homeland. I speak of the majority of peoples of South Africa who, because of the abominations of apartheid, live dispossessed of their rightful homes and homeland. I speak of the Palestinians, whose very legitimate name has become synonymous with the agony of forced, miserable exile, or refugee states under military occupation.

If we would love and serve justice, then we cannot wait for comfort and for comrades before we speak aloud, ourselves, on behalf of this manifold homelessness that tests the integrity of our conscience, right now.

Like running, trying to live a good life has to hurt a little bit, or we're not running hard enough, not really trying.

And if we want others, different from ourselves and stronger, perhaps, than we, to notice what we need when we cannot, ourselves, eliminate our neediness, then we must not, ourselves, attempt to live deaf and dumb to the clamor of human crying out that surrounds us. For no matter how desolate our own condition, there is someone else depending on our humanity for his or her rescue.

His or her is a careful distinction peculiar to our time, and Dr. King died before a movement emerged to include the existence of women in every thought pretending to be profound. But his own life followed that of Frederick Douglass and W. E. B. Du Bois, for example: two giants of American history who both took pains to acknowledge the legitimacy of women's aspirations for equality as well as the outstanding political contributions of Black women, in particular. And yet, one can find scant indication that Dr. King recognized the indispensable work of Black women within the Civil Rights Movement. On the contrary, there is no record of his gratitude for Ella Baker's intellectual leadership. There is no record of his seeking to shake the hand of Mrs. Fannie Lou Hamer.

And in this regard, I clearly do not believe that we should emulate the man who was not God.

Jo-Ann Robinson, Diane Nash, Rosa Parks, Ruby Doris Robinson, Septima Clarke, Bernice Reagon, Ella Baker, Fannie Lou Hamer, and, of course, Angela Davis: we should know the names and the important stories of the lives of these heroines of our epoch. They are just a handful of the amazing components of The Invisible Woman whose invisibility has cost all of us incalculable loss, and strategic and tactical error.

And the invisibility of women has furthermore cost *women* incalculable harm and sorrow.

But neither we who are women or that other 49 percent can afford this invisibility, because it's wrong, it's stupid, and—I hope I may confidently assert—*it's over.*

I believe that at least these extraordinary changes will follow from new insistent visibility and audibility of women in our political and moral lives:

1. When anyone speaks for or of the people, she will not fail *to attempt* to represent at least half of the human beings to whom she is responsible.

2. In addition to traditional concepts of politics as a public endeavor, the newly visible and audible women will introduce the feminist perspective of the personal as political. This will mean that the moral and political measurement of a life will not be taken only according to legislative outcome

of a campaign, or battlefield body counts after the battle. Moral measurement of a life will also happen hour by hour, and according to every single interpersonal episode.

3. In addition to the traditional concept of true commitment that means you are willing to die for what you think is right, we will make equal space for the womanly concept of commitment that means you are willing to live for what you believe, and for the sake of whatever it is that you love.

Where does all of this place me in respect to the mountain?

I feel I am privileged, indeed, to look at the mountain and to discover its influential presence in my life. I already know that a mountain is not a meadow or a farm or an ocean *or* a molehill. So I am fairly solid on my feet as I approach the mountain as a mountain.

And where does all of this place me in respect to the man who was not God?

I am thankful that he lived and that he loved us and that he tried so hard to be and do good.

I have come to understand and to dedicate myself to the community of his dream, the righteous revolution implied by his ardent reaching for economic and social justice.

As it is written in Isaiah 65:21–25:

They shall build houses and inhabit them;
they shall plant vineyards and eat their fruit.
They shall not build and another inhabit;
they shall not plant and another eat;
for like the days of a tree shall the days of my people be,
and my chosen shall long enjoy the work of their hands.
They shall not labor in vain,
or bear children for calamity;
for they shall be the offspring of the blessed of the Lord,
and their children with them.
Before they call I will answer,
while they are yet speaking I will hear.
The wolf and the lamb shall feed together,

the lion shall eat straw like the ox;
and dust shall be the serpent's food.
They shall not hurt or destroy
in all my holy mountain,
says the Lord.

And I have come to praise him, and to try to follow after Martin Luther King, Jr., this Black man of God as it is written in Matthew 5:11–12:

Blessed are you when men revile you and persecute you and utter all kinds of evil against you falsely on my account. Rejoice and be glad, for your reward is great in heaven, for so men persecuted the prophets who were before you.

I believe, I have faith, that the man who was not God will be *blessed* among men *and* women because

the effect of righteousness will be peace,
and the result of righteousness,
quietness and trust for ever.

Isaiah 32:17

Amen.

America
in Confrontation
with
Democracy,
or,
The Meaning of
the Jesse Jackson
Campaign

REVOLUTION ALWAYS UNFOLDS INSIDE AN ATMOSPHERE OF RIS-
ing expectations. Given the unexpected, hard-won success of
Jesse Jackson's 1988 presidential campaign, the Third American Revolution[1] may well be on its way. Certainly, the phenomenon of a Black man bidding for the most powerful office
in the world has raised, irreversibly, the expectations of Americans who, prior to Jackson's candidacy, never even dreamed
about accurate, or responsive, political representation. The
compelling personal history of Jesse Jackson must inspire the

This essay was originally published in the *Village Voice,* November 1988.
[1]The First American Revolution secured American independence from England. The
Second American Revolution broadly increased the civil rights of Black men and
women, America's largest minority.

least powerful and the most despised segments of our body politic. Born to an unwed teenage mother in South Carolina, Jackson came of age when no Black man or woman would ever request a public cup of coffee, or enter a public bathroom, or undertake to register to vote, without calculating the easily fatal risks attached to such a simple act. Jackson illuminates the value of an aggressive and rallying self-respect. In addition, his tendency to formulate policies on the basis of geopolitical facts rather than "the other way around," his fastening on justice as the touchstone for policy evaluation, have galvanized the otherwise dormant political energies of young and well-educated Americans from Berkeley, California, to Madison, Wisconsin.

I knew about Jesse and the U.S.A. because I travel across America, rather incessantly; at least once a week I am on a plane bound for some destination a thousand or more miles remote from New York City's Mayor Ed Koch or $275 monthly fees for parking your car in a garage. I knew about Jesse but I had suspended my thoughts about the impending election year of 1988; Jackson was going to surprise the hell out of a whole lot of people. I could sit back and wait for Jackson to break through media censorship.

But then, London surprised me. I could find no one among my internationalist new acquaintances who understood what was happening in my country. Jackson's name elicited vague looks or passionless questions about Minister Farrakhan, or angry gossip about caricature treatments of Jesse in the British press. Ultimately, he would emerge as a controversial, and entertaining, personality. No one supposed we might be talking about the possible next leader of "the Free World." Of course, London is not New York. But when I began to fathom the extent of British editorial obedience to America's *New York Times,* and NBC-TV, I got scared. My complacency seemed altogether unwarranted. And even though I could never have imagined the eventual determining power of New York riled against an American electorate in revolt, a power shamelessly revealed in April 1988, I returned to the States in considerable agitation. If national white media continued their de facto denial of his campaign, Jackson might really lose the game on grounds of fair play relentlessly circumvented for the purpose of defeating him.

Back home, I sought to convince a leading Black magazine of the good news growing up around Jesse's indefatigable, coast-to-coast campaign appearances. He really had a shot at the title; white Americans were listening to him, and they really liked most of what they heard. But we, Blackfolks, needed to jump in, fast, and get the word out: This was not some symbolic trial-run towards another sorry and foregone conclusion. Jackson could win!

But Black media dependency upon white media judgments prevailed. And, in addition, there were other impediments to early, independent Black media coverage that might have countered the intentionally soporific and paralyzing effects of white censorship:

1. Seven years of Ronald Reagan had not provided for the positive decline of racist habits or attitudes in America and yet Jackson's developing national triumph would seem to require, or to imply, just such a decline as a precondition for his victorious rise into national consciousness. The success of Jackson's campaign did not make sense and, therefore, could not, in fact, be happening.

2. On the other hand, if Jackson's appeal to white Americans depended upon coalitional thinking and work, if, for example, Jackson's broadening appeal resulted from his neglect, or diminution, of issues centered upon racial inequities (i.e., "Economic Justice" in place of "Racial Justice"), then *whose* candidate, whose representative was he, anyway? Was he "ours" or "theirs"?

If you stood, directly in front of Jesse Jackson while he propounded his programs for change, you could quiet these quandaries or answer these questions, but, otherwise, white media reporting on Jackson's campaign failed to disseminate even halfway fair, or accurate, accounts of his proposals, or live audience response to his ideas, until the very beginning of 1988.

In short, national white media colluded with Democratic party bosses to silence, to slander, and, finally, to stop Jesse Jackson. Black radio and print media executives, handicapped by comparatively meager resources in committing to Jackson's campaign in Minneapolis, Minnesota, or Fairbanks, Alaska, were slow to believe the good news that they could neither see nor hear for themselves, firsthand. White media moguls censored Jackson because they thought he just might accomplish "the impossible" and become the Democratic nominee. Black media executives moved their personnel too slowly into reporting positions in part because they could not believe his victory was possible or that his victory, won on national terms, would not compromise Jackson's wholehearted devotion to racist jeopardies with which Black Americans must contend.

But media apart, hundreds and then thousands and thousands of white and black Americans found themselves standing in front of this indisputably charismatic orator. From his own mouth they understood that, regardless of ethnic or regional or age identity, they would have to surrender nothing in order to gain a great deal: alliance need not produce merger or submergence. Even racist habits of mind became beside the point— you could vote for "the nigger" not because you wanted a Black man in your family but because you thought he might save your family farm. Counted multitudes of white Americans eschewed stupidities of racist reflex for the sake of their own self-interest. More and more listening Americans realized that you don't have to be Black to become "an outsider" in your own native land: our democracy.

At present, one major illness is enough to financially ruin and emotionally wreck a white middle-class family. Divorce or the death of a husband is enough to catapult a middle-class white woman and her children into poverty. One plant closing or relocation is enough to terminate the employment future of an entire city.

Twenty years after the assassination of Dr. Martin Luther King, Jr., the Reverend Jesse Jackson was standing up, by popular vote, the front-runner Democratic candidate for the presidency of the United States. This was the situation for more than half of the official primary season! He was standing on the principled vision of his predecessor, whose humanity had persuaded an awesome number of white Americans to reexamine their notions about "minority" and "majority" issues. Was hunger a Black problem or an American disgrace? Was equal access to good housing and education a Black demand or a necessity inside a democratic state? Was "Jobs or Income" an unreasonable, left-wing slogan or a matter of human survival?

I look upon the political phenomenon of Jesse Jackson as vindication of Dr. King's deepest faith in our collective potential as a democracy. And, what's more, Jackson's own radiant temerity in the face of negligible funding, press censorship, and attack has elicited the respect, and restored the activist self-respect, of a new American majority: a multiracial populist coalition of citizens intent upon the *humane* expansion of their citizen entitlements.

But Jesse did not only stand; he ran all over the place.

By the time the Democratic primary campaign became official, he was the only candidate who could say, "Next week *I'm going back* to talk with the farmers in Idaho. *I'm going back* to talk with the high school students of East Los Angeles about drugs. *I'm going back* to talk with the auto workers closed out of the factories in Detroit. *I'm going back* to talk with AIDS victims in San Francisco." He had been there. On picket lines, in living rooms—he had been everywhere, in America, again and again. He had left the National Rainbow Coalition meeting, October 1987, where he had declared himself an official candidate for the Democratic nomination, and he had flown directly to Washington, D.C., where he was *the only* Republican or Democratic contender for the U.S. presidency to appear. On that same day, in front of the Capitol building, Jackson had addressed a gay and lesbian rally attended by 600,000 Americans. He had supported gay and lesbian civil rights. He had demanded a colossal increase of federal funds to end the colossal scourge of AIDS. He had excoriated the sitting administration for its failure to protect homosexuals against discrimination, women against male violence, the American worker against economic violence perpetrated by corporate flight, and he was clearly just at the top of a long, long list of wrongs and remedies that, passionately and confidently, excluded nobody at all.

I remember a friend of mine telling me that when, in 1984, at the Democratic National Convention, Jesse spoke on behalf of lesbians, that moment was absolutely the first occasion on which she had heard "a politician say my name, he said the word, *lesbian*."

Jackson was the first presidential candidate, 1988, to plead and repeat the plight of 650,000 American farmers losing their farms within the eight years of Reagan's reign. He was the first to identify drugs as the number one menace to domestic security. He was the first and only American contender for the U.S. presidency to demand that South Africa be designated a terrorist state and treated accordingly. He was the first and only candidate to call the name of the Palestinian people; he said the words *the Palestinians,* and he called for self-determination, and statehood, for these beleaguered, taboo human beings. Jesse Jackson was the first and only candidate for the Democratic nomination to assert that there must be a single standard for the measurement, and protection, of human rights throughout the world: No country—not France nor Israel nor Nigeria nor South Korea nor Iran nor South Africa should be exempted from the requirements of that single standard. He was the first and only presidential contender to propose a world view profoundly alternative to the traditions of imperialist perspective.

Jackson proposed that the majority of human life / the peoples of the Third World be accorded proportionate political respect, economic aid, and inventive consideration as potential social and economic partners. No longer should the Third World serve as a playpen for greedy, killer interventionist maneuvers by aging cold warriors. *And* he was the first and the only Republican or Democratic candidate to propose an international minimum wage.

Obviously, Jackson could have proposed these many things plus the obliteration of the moon and none of it, none of his isolated and courageous and visionary ideas, would have mattered but for the huge national endorsement he received.

After the "stunning" (March 26, 1988) Jackson victory in Michigan, where he took 55 percent of the votes and delivered a 2–1 defeat to Michael Dukakis, the currently powerful went crazy. America was out of (their) control. He had to be stopped.

Rivers of money rushed into the coffers of the Dukakis camp. Top Democratic party officials rid themselves of every pretense at neutrality/at letting "the people" choose their candidate. "Super-delegates" (i.e., nonelected persons invested with voting power at the Democratic National Convention and accountable only to Democratic party officials likewise operating "above" the irksome fray of determination by popular vote) found themselves besieged by party demands for preconvention commitment to Dukakis, whether or not he emerged as the popular-vote choice of "the people." Nobody dared to claim that Dukakis represented anything in particular or that he could reliably arouse anything more than a snore, but that was not the point. In the media, the message quickly telescoped into Vote for Dukakis or . . . and here the message tended to become diffuse and difficult, in fact, to summarize: Or what?

And despite the concerted rallying of the formidable host of Jackson's enemies after Michigan, he proceeded, one week later, to win more votes in Wisconsin (a state with less than 4 percent total Black population) than Gary Hart in 1984, when Hart carried Wisconsin. America was out of (their) control.

In the teeth of his winning populist support, national white media based in New York, or Washington, D.C., released hysterical cover headlines such as "What Does Jesse Want?" or, *ad nauseam,* they broadcast clearly invalid "expert" opinions to the effect that Jackson was "unelectable"—a disgusting neologism invented specifically to discredit Jackson's gathering success. They cut him off during televised debates. They stressed his "lack of experience." They referred to his dependency upon the Black vote (as though the Democratic party, itself, could win anything without the Black vote, and as though Alaska and Vermont were strongholds of Black populations rather than white snow). When none of these tactics worked, they insinuated that Jackson's good looks must point to marital infidelity (although, as it happens, there was no evidence forthcoming for such envious suppositions). And they attempted to clear the mythical American mainstream of his contamination: he was "radical" and "harebrained" and "naïve," even though American opinion polls taken during

Reagan's reign repeatedly showed, for example, most Americans opposed to intervention in Central America, and opposed to collaboration with Pretoria. Most Americans favored exactly those federal programs of social support that Reagan tried to eviscerate, or eliminate altogether. Most Americans viewed official policies of deceit and constitutional evasion as hazardous to our national health.

Jesse was swimming in the mainstream alongside a new American majority: a populist, politically unrepresented, politically uncontrollable mass of angry and needful and internationally embarrassed white and Black, rural and urban, straight and gay American citizens. He had to be stopped.

But none of the multiple outraged interests arrayed against him were eager to say why. That revelation could simply add millions to Jackson's already dangerous score. Then how would they do it?

Racism could not kill the Jackson campaign. If you pumped hard enough, you could probably find some jackass willing to say he'd be damned if he'd "let the niggers hold a barbecue on the White House lawn." But any rational analysis of the outcome of the Democratic primaries makes it clear that Jackson's racial identity did not and could not defeat him in the voting booth.

American powers threatened by the content and the constituency of Jackson's campaign had little to do with asinine prejudice or any other emotional disorder: Antidemocratic-politics-as-usual and the Democratic national party and multinational corporations and the American banking community and the American Medical Association and the Pentagon and right-wing fundamentalists rightly assessed Jackson's explosive arrival as a comprehensive, coherent, programmatic, moral, and populist rejection of government unrelated to the welfare of the governed, of labor at the mercy of "the marketplace," of the sick kneeling to those who should heal them, of the weak systematically abandoned to the streets and the bully violence of random/crackpot America.

He had to be stopped. And, measured by the number of delegates at stake, the next, the pivotal, battleground would be New York. This was where Jackson's enemies needed to break the neck of his campaign. But how? I think it looked easy. In New York you had the largest Jewish community outside of Israel, constituting 23 percent of the voting electorate. You had a big-time lunatic in the office of the mayor. You had the *New York Times,* which saw fit to publish only one Black op-ed throughout the Democratic primary season. You had the national headquarters of *Time* magazine, *Newsweek,* NBC-TV, and so forth. The showdown was set. The goal was burial of a startling upstart.

Ah, Israel. Such a tiny sovereign state, with fewer inhabitants than the New York City borough of Brooklyn. Could you reduce a national, populist uprising, and its leader, to one issue, the issue of Israel? Well, evidently. But here the clouds converge and blur and mist falls and general miasma overtakes the public brain. What "issue," exactly?

It seems that Jesse thought that the "parties-in-conflict"— the Israelis and the Palestinians—ought to negotiate their differences directly with each other. It seems that Jesse thought that the Palestinian people should have somewhere other than atrocious "refugee camps" to live. It seems that Jesse thought that human rights do not lose their relevance whenever any of us decide we detest somebody else.

Jackson avowed and reiterated his abhorrence of anti-Semitism, as well as racism, and homophobia. He affirmed his commitment to the security of Israel. He thought, he said more than once, that peaceful relations with your neighbors would better assure national security than armed occupation. He did

not, he never addressed the spectacle of human rights violations carried out by Israeli occupation forces in the West Bank
and Gaza Strip, simultaneous with the battle for the Democratic nomination. He did not, he never asserted that Israel,
along with South Africa, should be declared "a terrorist state,"
and treated accordingly. And meanwhile, from January 1988
to April 19, 1988, Israeli armed forces and Israeli "settlers"
adopted a "broken bones policy" of repression, and they furthermore broke down doors, tear-gassed pregnant women,
buried Palestinians alive, closed more than eight hundred
schools in the West Bank, deported several Palestinians without trial, arrested and indefinitely detained thousands of Palestinians without trial, demolished homes, "closed" Palestinian
towns, and killed more than two hundred Palestinian men,
women, and children—none of them armed.

Early in 1988, the U.S. Congressional Black Caucus composed and publicly released a position paper challenging the
logic whereby Israel receives more U.S. aid than any other
foreign country in the world, on unconditional terms. But this
was the Congressional Black Caucus, not Jesse Jackson.

Jackson did publicly question the meaning of Israel's military, nuclear, and commercial partnership with South Africa.
And what about that?

In New York State, where 25 percent of the electorate is
Black, where more than 40,000 Americans live homeless,
where drug dealing and drug addiction terrorize every neighborhood, where bridges collapse and subways defy your tolerance for filth, and where public schools fail to keep most of
their students and also fail to teach those who stay, what was
"the issue of Israel"?

The media made it happen. Television and newspaper com-
mentators never tired of raising "the key question," as they
were pleased to term it: What was Jackson's relationship to the
Jews? According to the media, this was not only "the key

question," this was the sole question for examination. And then, New York City's mayor, Edward Koch, saved the ugly day: "Jews Would Be Crazy to Vote for Jackson," he declared. And, having determined the question, the media now brandished "the answer." Page one/top of the TV news/ubiquitous to the eyes and ears of New York residents, the fight for the Democratic party's nomination for the presidency of the United States had become a media-induced fight between two minorities: Jews and Blacks.

As they say in New York, "very nice."

Except for notably brave and outspoken Jewish dissent from this hate-mongering formulation—dissent by Rabbi Balfour Brickner, the group calling itself Jews for Jackson, and Barry Feinstein, head of New York City's Teamsters' Union, and, at the last minute, Norman Mailer, who endorsed Jackson one day before the New York primary on the op-ed page of the *Times*—the national Jewish community kept silent.

The Democratic national party kept silent. New York's governor Mario Cuomo said nothing. In response to the abominable blatherings by Mayor Ed Koch, there was no editorial outcry in the *New York Times* or on TV. Evidently you could not affirm the humanity of Palestinians, but you could abuse your public office to impugn the sanity of any Jewish man or woman who might choose to support Jesse Jackson.

Within this inflamed, special-case scenario of New York and the Democratic primaries, on April 19, 1988, Jesse took New York City, and virtually all of New York's Black and Hispanic vote. He did not win the Jewish vote. And, he lost the state. To win, he would have needed Democratic national party support at least commensurate to his demonstrated "electability," and he would have needed a mass-media environment that succumbed neither to the manipulations of a non-issue-one-issue alarm, nor to the pressures of cowardly power afraid to publicly duke it out with Jackson.

By the evening of April 19, 1988, Jackson had already won Democratic primary contests in Alabama, Georgia, Louisiana, Mississippi, Virginia, Texas, Alaska, South Carolina, Puerto Rico, Michigan, the Virgin Islands, and Delaware. On that same infamous April 19 of his New York State defeat, Jackson won the primary election in Vermont. And, several weeks after April 19, or Scam Tuesday in New York, the *New York Times* published these findings on the State of the Democratic race: as of May 5, the new front-runner, Michael Dukakis, had received 6,689,305 popular votes, or 37 percent of the total votes cast, while Jackson had won 5,079,263, or 28 percent. There was less than a 10 percent popular barrier between Jackson's hopes and Jackson's victory.

If he had taken New York State, Jackson's nomination by the Democratic party would have been assured—unless the Democrats had decided to mutilate their own rules (not unlikely) or California voters had opted for Dukakis a month before the Democratic convention in July (very unlikely).

It was that close. He had almost made it. And nobody knew how close Jackson had come to changing American history better than his most devoted enemies. He had already changed our history, and they knew it. With no money, and no Democratic party support remotely proportional to his demonstrated "electability," Jesse Jackson had emerged, the most familiar, popular, and small-*d* democratic candidate in the public mind and eye. But, New York had cost him the Democratic party's nomination.

The rest is not history. America is not the same old anything it was, prior to the 1988 leadership of Jesse Jackson. The reasons for a Third American Revolution have not gone away. The needs of all the Americans who propelled Jackson to the front of our own uprising have not been met. Our distinctively humane values have neither been erased from our hearts nor honored by those who scramble to maintain power over our lives. New York is not the U.S.A.: we persist, neither stupid nor satisfied.

And, we have not lost the war.

Jackson has transformed the nature and the substance of acceptable political discourse in America. Even the Republican presidential candidate, George Bush, will struggle to enunciate metaphors about "a thousand points of light" while his narrow eyes sting and water from his own rhetoric about "a kinder, gentler nation." And the keynote speaker at the Republican convention, Thomas Kean, governor of New Jersey, apparently felt it necessary to assert, "We will search out bigotry and racism—we will drag it into the sunshine of understanding and make it wither and die."

Up against Dukakis and the Democratic party, Jackson set the agenda for the platform debate. And, while many of the demands of his program met with resolute derision, he did succeed in gaining the Democratic party's designation of South Africa as a terrorist state, and he did push Dukakis into a posture of unequivocal opposition to aid to the contras, unequivocal support for child care, and, alas, equivocal support for universal health insurance. He did embarrass the Democrats into public refusal to establish a "no first strike" nuclear policy, and he did force the Democratic Party to reduce by 50 percent the number of "Super-delegates" who will be anointed for the next presidential election campaign. He did, irreversibly, tutor American consciousness about the continuing anti-democratic political structures that block our decisive exercise of the vote, and he did, again, embarrass Dukakis into publicly waffling on Dukakis's own promise to fund a nationwide voter registration drive and to vastly simplify the whole voting registration process. He did lead the reentry of concepts of right and wrong back into the center of political deliberations. He did meet with Israel's ambassador to the United States, August

8, 1988, and Israel's ambassador to the United States did meet, August 8, 1988, for more than two hours, with the Reverend Jesse Jackson, and, you know, Jesse just really came really, really close to opening up the White House to the world's best barbecue and general/populist celebration of all time.

And as for those millions and millions of us who chose Jesse Jackson as our candidate, we would have to be deaf, dumb, and blind not to notice how much we scared the currently powerful: literally, we scared them almost to death!

FINDING THE WAY HOME

EVERY THREE YEARS, "ALL OF AMERICA" MOVES OUT OF TOWN. As this new year begins, I find myself inside that privileged mainstream of nomadic Americans. I am looking for a better place to live. I am choosing between climates, predictable colors of the sky, racial and ethnic mixtures among possible colleagues or neighbors, artistic or intellectual communities in place, available political camaraderie, and the financial and physical costs of housing in relationship to work. I am trying to find my way home.

Two-and-a-half years ago, I forever abandoned the homogeneous, street-deserted, house-bound, heterosexist desperation of the Long Island suburbs and returned to my beloved Brooklyn where, I knew, my eyes and ears would never be lonely for diversified, loud craziness and surprise. But tonight I am exhausted by routine danger and the price tag attached to my single life-style. I am no longer amused by the six-block walk between the garage where I must park my car and the building where I must climb three flights of (carpeted) stairs before I can

This essay was originally published in *The Progressive*, February 1989.

enter my own living room. But, mostly, I am seeking an escape from answering-machine ellipses and the need to take an exorbitant taxi before you can sit beside a lover or a friend. I want a surrounding of lovers and friends. I want that safety. I want safety that I do not have to purchase at the expense of a healthy personal life.

And so, following the average American clock to the minute, I think I will probably move somewhere new by the middle of 1989. In the meantime, in my wondering, wandering heart, in my fearful and hungry state of acute disequilibrium, I am homeless. But I am overloaded with privilege. I am wracked by real-life options that transmit the same amazing message: You can choose where you will live. You can cut and run or fly and stop and land in a happier spot than the one that you now occupy.

Having settled my own intimate objectives for the new year, it is not difficult to identify related political issues that I must engage. This is my short list: for 1989 I dedicate myself to the memory of Lisa Steinberg and to the future of the Palestinian people.

Six-year-old Lisa really is dead. Did anyone ever show her an old-fashioned storybook of fireside evenings on the hearth with Mom and Dad and Brother and Sleeping Dog practically comatose with tender contentment? Or how about a television series showing cops and teachers and other kids from down the hall and rabbis and social workers and rock stars and poets and doctors and lawyers and mayors and governors berserk with outrage and speeding with determination and setting up benefits and tearing down doors and holding a solitary beaten child very very close to their hearts? Did she ever see that? She did not.

There was nowhere for her to go. There was no one worthy of her inevitable trust. She could neither invent nor discover her own safety, her own benign environment. The bottom-line translation of child abuse means that Lisa Steinberg lived and died homeless in America.

I refuse coexistence with the unspeakable indictment of that fact. And whatever it takes, telegrams to legislators/hammer and nails/bodily intervention/money through the mail/regular bouts of "babysitting" at-large or, yes, adoption, per se, I am resolved to save at least one child from the violence of our insanity and neglect. To this end, I will be searching for relevant comrades and group initiatives to support.

In the meantime, on the eve of Yasir Arafat's courageous "We want peace. We want peace. We are committed to peace. We are committed to peace. We want to live in our Palestinian state, and let live" statement in Geneva, the Israeli government "confined" 650,000 Palestinians to their "homes" and cut off the electricity. The bottom line for six million Palestinian men, women, and children is that they are living and they are dying, homeless, in full view of the whole world. I refuse coexistence with the unspeakable indictment of that fact.

But where is the outcry against the murder of more than three hundred Palestinians subjected to the fatal caprice of military occupation? Where is the evidence of horror and moral and political mobilization when any single Palestinian is shot and killed "by accident," or otherwise? Who among us would accommodate to an absence of civil liberties or no control over the light switch in our house? Who would accept military proscription of the funeral services for any member of our family?

I believe that the issue of a home for Lisa Steinberg and the issue of a home for the Palestinian people are one and the same: the question is whether non-Europeans and whether children, everywhere, possess a human right to sanctuary on this planet.

And so, no matter where and when I move again, I will be

working with everything I've got to change the apparent answer that obtains today. As Buckminster Fuller once said, "Man is not a tree." We have no excuse. We are neither ignorant nor fundamentally inert, except, of course, by choice.

Wrong

or

White

We enter this last-ditch decade of the twentieth century still staggering from the final revolutionary events of 1989. The astounding spectacle of millions of people in bodily rejection of terror and the abrogation of their human rights must summon each of us from our most cynical inertia. If you missed out on "the Sixties," well, then, here in a brief three or four weeks you could witness entirely comparable, gigantic, and spontaneous maneuvers initiated by ideas of freedom. From Germany to Rumania, a colossal rout of institutional and other tyrannies took place.

And it was white on white: East Germans rushing to embrace West Germans, or Nicolae Ceausescu versus the hundreds of thousands of Rumanians who surged forward to depose him, or Mikhail Gorbachev forced to respond to a Lithuanian challenge to Soviet rule. Nobody powerful in the U.S.A., neither the politicians nor their media echo-men, chose to condemn or chide or advise or trivialize or ignore or threaten or misrepresent or patronize any of these anarchic

This essay was originally published in *The Progressive,* February 1990.

and mysterious, and, yes, ultimate and sometimes deadly confrontations with a demeaning and cruel status quo. No American with national access to network cameras elected to
characterize these wild explosions of fury and unrest as "mob
hysteria" or "terrorist" or "lawless" or "riotous" or "violent"
or "subversive" and, indeed, the word "communist" suddenly
became an adjective equivalent to "tall" or "fat"—as in, "the
tall (or fat or communist) shoemaker opened the door." It was
white on white.

From Germany to Hungary to Czechoslovakia to Poland to
Rumania, the *intifada* of an uncontrollable and hopeful and
raging multitude again and again erupted and then proceeded
to its own German or Hungarian or Czechoslovakian or Polish
or Rumanian destiny: neither the Americans nor the Soviets
interfered or intervened through overt or covert means. And
the Berlin Wall came down. It was white on white.

Unfettered by superpower ideology or manipulation, these
localized struggles for autonomy and civil liberties unfolded,
day by day. You could see the kindred victories of different
peoples left to their own judgments and need. It was white on
white.

None of these ordinary heroes would be sneeringly identified as Arabs or Palestinians. They were Poles. Those uproari-
ous hordes overthrowing demands for visas and checkpoint
inspections and submission to massive, actual barriers to freedom—they were not seeking to overcome the confinements of
apartheid. They were Germans. The people chanting beneath
the palace balconies—they did not speak Spanish, they were
not citizens of Nicaragua or El Salvador or Panama. These
victims of their own passivity and these victories against the
docile spirit that allows a tyrant or a tyranny to stand among
their lives—these were European components of European
history under populist siege. It was white on white. It was
right, whatever it was. It was white on white.

And analyzing this European drama, and speaking to the European multitudes here, and there, it was white on white: white men of the American press corps telling the world whatever white European spokesmen told them about what this or that revolutionary scenario meant or did not mean. And, whether spoken in English or shouted out in an unfamiliar European language, the slogans that lifted the arms and the fists and the hearts and the heads of the millions of revolutionaries who would no longer tolerate what has become everywhere intolerable—those slogans carried my own heart back to America, back to a time when we knew what was wrong, when we knew we were right: from our own historic mass demonstrations for "Free-dom Free-dom!" to "Black Power!" to "Make Love Not War!" to the San Francisco candlelight vigil for the meaning of the murdered life of Harvey Milk to the Take Back the Night demonstrations for the safety of women. Like an avalanche of extremely tender memories, these American images of humane revolt engulfed my mind and I could think and feel, at last, a brotherhood and sisterhood of unity with those European strangers enflamed by revolutionary faith and herding themselves into their own new, invincible, and righteous light.

And I noticed that none of the American news media moguls described these astounding developments as "bad" or "dangerous." I noticed that, consistently, from the Oval Office to NBC-TV, these overwhelming facts of European *intifada* came across to us, the regular people of the U.S.A., as unequivocal good news. It was white on white.

It was really striking. Over there, in Europe, as a matter of fact, you could watch the surprise and the lightning speed of structural change that we, Americans of the 1980s, had come to regard as impossible or, at best, as something that the military would or should "quell." Where were the Marines, for God's sake?

And, meanwhile, U.S. support of death-squad government in El Salvador did not abate. U.S. imposition of millions of dollars intended to rig upcoming elections in Nicaragua did not stop. The administration's and the media's concessions to phony questions about the legitimacy of the leadership of the ANC in South Africa and the PLO on the Gaza Strip and the West Bank—these disgusting tactics of racist oppression—they did not wane or disappear.

These were matters of wrong and white. These issues and broken bones and broken laws and children killed and sovereignty denied and villages brutally occupied—these did not contain the same somehow sacred and intrinsically democratic principles at stake: not the same as East and West Berlin; not white on white; not possibilities for great news. El Salvador, South Africa, Israel—these were categorically different situations of wrong and white. Your nation, your family, your face was neither European nor of European descent. You were wrong. And whether it was Washington, D.C., or Jerusalem, or Pretoria, the wisdom and the virtue and the military force to correct and control your misbegotten miserable existence would be and would remain white power.

It was really striking. And I remembered things. I remembered U.S. obsessions with purported monster-types like Muammar Qaddafi and Yasir Arafat and Manuel Noriega. I remembered Israeli references to Palestinian people as "beasts with two legs." And I sat reading American newspapers that now, and abruptly, informed me about somebody in Rumania, a white man named Nicolae Ceausescu whose regime had slaughtered more than 60,000 Rumanian men and women, and I wondered: How come the CIA never sent big bucks and probably Rambo himself to topple that atrocious government? How come the U.S. Marines never did anything to "establish democracy" in the context of that European government? But I knew why. It was just another matter of wrong and white.

Neither Qaddafi nor Arafat nor Noriega is a white man. And too bad about that.

Meanwhile, there were women still living on the planet. If you looked closely at the televised crowd scenes in revolutionary Eastern Europe, you could see them, right there, mixed up with the rest of "the people": the white men who would, sooner or later, explain to everybody what was obvious and then say why they, or why some of these white men, would soon replace other white men in the vestments of state power.

And, elsewhere, in El Salvador, the U.S.-supported death squads of Alfredo Cristiani had assassinated six Jesuit priests, plus "a cook and her fifteen-year-old daughter." Okay, no names/no "human-interest" angle/no appropriately reverential feature stories, but what could you expect? Neither that cook nor her fifteen-year-old daughter ever attended a single revolutionary-committee meeting, never received a proper invitation to participate in such a gathering, never learned how to handle an M-16 or hold a political-rally microphone, and anyway, we're talking about one woman and a girl.

And, back home in Berkeley, where I live, some women graduate students had organized a rally against U.S. intervention in El Salvador, and that rally was to be held in People's Park. And it was. It happened just a few days after a white man murdered fourteen young women who were students at the School of Engineering at the University of Montreal. They were there, these young women, mixed up with the rest of the students. And this particular white man looked very closely at the students in order to find the women. He ordered the men to one side of a room and the women to the other side. He allowed the men to leave. Then he shot and killed fourteen women. I think all of them were white. I know they were women. I know that they died because they were not young white men in that school of engineering. Reportedly, before he pulled the trigger fourteen times, this particular young white man screamed at his female prey. Reportedly, he screamed that they were "all a bunch of fucking feminists."

None of those fourteen young white women was a white man. And too bad about that.

So, at this People's Park rally on El Salvador, the turnout was not terrific. El Salvador is not white. As I stood, waiting my turn to speak to the small and scattered audience, I was chatting with two or three of the young white women organizers. And, suddenly, a particular Black man approached us at a methodical, slow pace. As he came abreast of our group, he raised his hands and struck me and the young woman immediately next to me, attempting to knock both of us down. Enraged, I instantly retaliated with a blow between his shoulder blades and, I noticed, he decided not to repeat himself in gratuitous assault upon myself or any other woman on the premises.

And then, as part of her introduction of me, another young white woman asked for a moment of silence to commemorate the murder of the fourteen young white women in Montreal. Some of us kept silent. I could hear the voices of a variety of young men and older men defiling that one hushed minute. And a passionate confusion of aims overtook my mind: Where was the battleground? El Salvador? People's Park? The University of Montreal?

And I could not sort my way among these urgencies. And I refused to choose among these horrors, these attacks on freedom and autonomy and life itself.

I am not a white man. I am not a man. I get emotional about these things—the invasion of my space, my body. I get really upset when somebody kills fourteen human beings because they are not men. I become hysterical when a sexist double standard means nobody totally blows away business as usual whenever any woman is terrorized or raped or murdered.

And I really don't give a damn whether it's one cook and her daughter or one unidentified young Black woman or fourteen young white women on a university campus in Montreal, or myself, standing around in Berkeley's People's Park. The sexist double standard that would have us accept that we should not wail aloud and storm the streets on behalf of our own safety, our own womanly, our own female self-determination, well, to hell with that, from Montreal to Rumania, to hell with that.

I am not "a divisive issue." I am not page 12 material. I want the liberty and the hallowed, full human rights of every woman in the world at the top of the news, right there, mixed up with the East Berliners rushing to embrace the people of West Berlin. And I want this new decade to forswear all double standards. No more of this one standard for white people and then there's Panama. No more "establishment of democracy" courtesy of the U.S. Army. No more official regret for the death toll of "American lives." No more "unknown numbers" of "unidentified" and officially ignored victims of white power. I demand the names of every Panamanian man and woman and child who died because George Bush could not have a merry Christmas unless he tried to eliminate Manuel Noriega, who was trying his best to act like a colored white man with an army at his disposal!

The racist premises for American domestic and foreign policy persist in obscene nudity today. And who is celebrating what, exactly, in Berlin or Poland or Czechoslovakia? And after the huge shopping spree in West Germany, and after the huge, revolutionary glee of Eastern Europe dissipates, and after Archbishop Desmond Tutu returns from his on-site protest against Israeli apartheid to South Africa, and after who wins what electoral office in Nicaragua because of or despite the infusion of millions of American dollars, and after the latest hollow man has been propped into place by U.S. troops in Panama City, there will still be women living on the planet.

There are many wars going on and one of them is universal and it's gender-specific against my particular, non-European, and female presence in the world and so I'm watching TV, you know, and making these notes, and I'm thinking to myself that it's not only necessary, it's possible to end these dictatorships that hate my guts. But, probably, I will have to turn off the TV, even though it's fabulous and fascinating to see how, white on white, a righteous revolution will materialize if people are just left, respectfully, alone to determine where and when they will formulate the deal as "win or die."

And I believe that Rumania can happen here. I believe that the Berlin Wall of psychopathic racism and psychopathic misogyny will fall apart or America will die. It's not complicated. We have no choice. Ours is not a nation-state of white on white. And we are not a country of men!

It's 1990. And one of these next mornings I'm gonna rise up and rush right into America and if you look closely you will be able to see me from as far away as Czechoslovakia and I'm not gonna get weary and I'm not gonna give up until it's safe to be here, where I was born, where I belong.

But what will that take?

Unrecorded Agonies

THE LONG-NEGLECTED ANIMAL ROSE UP, JERKED FREE FROM
regular control, and shook itself alert and furious. The long-
neglected animal began to growl and shake and howl and
shake and, shuddering, became a beast incapable of slow or
soft or satiate and, suddenly, in rabid revolution rising with
jaws wide and ears flat to the risen hair, the long-neglected
animal howls at the silence of too many years abused and
hungry; too many years of cowering in arrangements with
patterns of contempt; too many years of too much burden
carelessly laid upon its back.

5:05 p.m., Berkeley, California, October 17, 1989.

I am returning from an upright idyll in the Berkeley hills, a
solitary four-mile walk among flowers and under trees so fra-
grant I can feel myself intoxicated as I dream about a young
Black woman, nineteen years old, who never moved among
such commonplace and public smells and colors thriving easily. She lived in Brooklyn and she died there, gang-raped on a
Brooklyn roof and thrown off, thrown down, screaming but
inaudible. Her unrecorded, unremembered murder joined her
to the legions of Black women whose demise, whose violated

This essay was originally published in *The Progressive,* December 1989.

bodies never lead to rallies/marching/vigilante vendettas/legis-
lation/loudspeaker-scale memorial services/determined prosecution and community revenge.

I had been dreaming about her, this "unidentified victim" of
my own neglect. I would. I thought, compose an unforgivably
belated tribute, "Requiem for What's-Her-Name," supposing
I could rouse myself from such environmental languor as the
California hills at sunset frequently induce.

My feet could not find the ground. I had been stepping off the
curb to cross the street and then my right foot hovered in a
terrifying new infinity of space. There was no ground below
me. The earth tilted violent and absolute. I thought, "This is
it; this is the end of all of it." I stretched out my arms struggling
for balance, for flight. Under me, nothing held together. In
front of my eyes, the world slipped to a dizzying diagonal. And
then a shuddering convulsed my body and the neighborhood
around me, and I felt a roaring, and I sensed the madness of
apocalypse. And with the shuddering, the one word *earthquake* finally occurred to me: this was that flash quivering of
catastrophe to which all difference must submit; this was the
possibility of death in universal brief.

It stopped. Perhaps fifteen seconds had elapsed. The inside
of my head was reeling and ringing. I wanted to throw up.
Now the plentiful and thriving trees changed characters and
menaced my own safety: Would they fall on me as I passed
underneath them, inching my way home? Against my racing
heart, I slowly picked my steps towards the front door of my
home. Inside, pictures hung askew or had fallen to the floor.
Tapes, CDs, and books lay scattered. Two candleholders on
the dining-room table trembled out loud, incessantly. But I was
still alive. I could see and hear everything. I turned on the TV.

Game three of the World Series had been preempted by God.
Power was out. Phones were out. The TV stations ran on

batteries or generator equipment. A photo of the Bay Bridge kept taking over the screen. A fifty-foot span of the bridge had fallen. Cars had fallen. Water was leaking. Gas was leaking. Houses were falling. Houses and other buildings crumbled and fell. Fires started up. Fire spread. A mile-long section of the 880 freeway in Oakland collapsed. Hundreds of motorists had been trapped and crushed and killed. There was no electricity.

This was a 6.5 earthquake. No, a 6.7. No, a 7.0. This was a 7.0 earthquake. This was major. This was huge. Nothing since 1906 had seized and consumed and deranged and terrorized and endangered and incinerated and maimed and wrecked what is called "the San Francisco Bay Area."

A million calls a minute reached for the voices of the survivors. Circuits jammed. The heart of the living beat hard and very fast as aftershocks and secondary tremors passed through the terrain, rumbling and swaying to destabilize the earth. Nowhere felt steady.

I groped outside and, hand over hand against the outside wall of the house, I attempted to find the gas valve: "Turn off the gas! Do not smoke or light any fire! Turn off the gas!"

In San Francisco, somebody on the twenty-eighth floor of an office building thought she had died, already, as the structure rocked back and forth. And a young mother picking up her infant daughter from a day-care center literally picked her up and clasped her to her chest as glass broke and glass flew everywhere. From Candlestick Park Stadium, police evacuated 62,000 baseball fans. And now the Marina section of the city, a posh waterfront settlement of older homes, caught fire and blazed into oblivion and there was no obvious, no regular means to escape: the Bay Bridge was down and the Bay Bridge was closed and it was hours before anyone figured out alternative routes out of the stricken city.

The sun was gone. Below, the usual night-blossom of Berkeley lights had disappeared. The lights that remained gave the appearance of airport runways: geometric strings around vast patchworks of darkness. Across the Bay was nothing whatsoever. There was no light in that dark envelope of horror and tragic surprise.

And because the network TV studios are clustered in San Francisco, and despite the fact that the epicenter of the earthquake lay some fifty miles to the south of San Francisco, and although, in fact, the overwhelming great loss of human life befell the city of Oakland, and because there were no phones and mobility routes for cars and trucks, and because everyone concentrated on what he or she could see or hear for himself or herself, the world was learning about the fallen Bay Bridge and the colossal fires of San Francisco and the ungovernable destruction of property, and the old and the new homeless, and none of this was wrong or less than stupefying, less than awesomely chaotic. But, also, and really, from the first minutes forward we knew—even if no one remembered and even if no one mobilized about what we knew—we knew, we heard, we even saw by dint of aerial photography, we saw the smashed mile tombstone of the 880 Cypress Street Freeway in Oakland where, we were told, at least 274 human beings perished within fifteen seconds, they perished in a paroxysm of unrecorded agony.

It was 10:30 P.M. before I realized I did not have to sit by myself, inert. I am not a paramedic, but I have a press card. And even though city officials were begging everybody to stay off the streets and roads, that didn't necessarily mean "me": I could get up and get out and make some kind of eyewitness, or try.

Berkeley was silent. The streets were silent. Here and there a streetlamp had crashed to the ground and policemen in police cars gathered behind fuchsia pink flares gushing up pitiful bits of smoke. God, it was dark. Well-kept single-family houses sat quietly to the side and the car sped into the night.

I kept thinking as I glanced at block after block of thoughtful shelter and mowed lawns. I kept thinking how easily there could be no human life; how small the gestures of lovers and the living must seem inside the galaxies of our complete but burning universe; how slight a hand is love; how heavy is the deathblow to a life.

And there we were, my friend and I, outside the Emporium Capwell, a square-block department store in downtown Oakland. Private security guards stood about, whispering to each other, or not saying anything anymore. It looked as though the structure had sustained hours of artillery attacks. Every one of the street-level display windows lay pulverized and glinting bright on the sidewalks. Nude mannequins landed upside down in the darkness. A young Latino man in service uniform was sweeping the glass, his back to the torn-out section of the building where ordinarily he would not be able to afford to shop.

"How long have you been here?" I asked.

He shrugged and gave me a smile as sweet as Nicaragua.

"How long will you work, tonight?"

"I don't know," he answered me. "I work until they tell me I can go."

The security guards were Black. The workers sweeping up the mess appeared to be Latinos. The man inside the ruined store, the man taking inventory and ordering people about in the desolate rubble, was white.

We left the Emporium Capwell and sped toward 880. Police barricaded access to the site. Behind the barricades, card tables with emergency first-aid supplies wobbled under their load but stood ready. Stretchers waited, side by side. Ambulance sirens sounded the burst of sorrow, and the ambulances and the rescue trucks and the tractors and the fire engines and the police on motorcycles and the TV and print-media people in their passenger cars circled and parked and circled and looked and halted and waited and circled, and there were no sightseers anywhere, and there was no eating of apples or playing a boombox or smoking a cigarette, but couples held hands and people spoke in hushed fashion and stepped, gingerly, closer and closer, and you felt the commanding commonly somber response of teenagers and Black construction workers and Black and white policemen and the mixed paramedic rescue squads, and it was all the same quiet because we were all the same, finally, in this place of death.

But everyone wanted to help, and there was nothing to do. There was no help from this implacable and grisly harm around us. Ahead, we could see what remained of the mile-long 880 freeway: the viciously undulated steel. Some thing, some beast had stomped on the two-deckered highway, stomped it and squeezed it flat and buckled the concrete and ripped out the steel reinforcements and clawed them and battered them and broken concrete apart and snapped this enormous superstructure carrying commuters home on October 17, 1989, in Oakland, California. And I did not think any of us was meant to see the intestines of any highway, and I did not suppose that any of us was meant to perish in such a sudden but crushing collapse of our supports.

There was no fear in the night in that proximity to that mangled occasion for so much grief. We wanted to rescue anybody. We wanted to hear a call, a cry, a weeping to which we could respond. In fact, there was a crawlspace somewhere in that ruin, and Black and white men again and again risked their own lives climbing on that twisted steel and concrete seeking survivors. And they did, at one moment, come upon a six-year-old boy whose mother and father had been crushed in the front seat of their car, and the boy would reach forward to stroke his dead mother's face now and then, and the doctors said they would have to cut through the boy's mother to rescue the boy, and what did rescue mean anymore, and some of the remnants of victim vehicles indicated that the mile-long collapse of 880 had leveled some of the passenger cars to six inches flat and some otherwise crushed trucks compressed to two feet, and who were we looking for, what were we hoping to hear?

After a while, my friend and I left that vigil, and we drove through the crumbling corridors of west Oakland to find the hospital nearest to the collapsed section of 880.

At 1 A.M., the Public Information Officer looks as though three pounds of tears are packed and pushing hard behind her barely open eyes: Phyllis Brown is a petite Black woman whose soft-spoken and deliberate manner absolutely blends into the remarkable calm and orderliness of the emergency room where she has been on duty, now, for sixteen hours, and she is tired but steady as a nurse prepared to calm and ease whatever the suffering may require.

"We have been running on emergency mode since 5:15," she explains, "and until two hours ago we had no lights." She tightens her lips slightly, and then she concludes: "It has been difficult."

Around us, as we stand, staff people move about almost silently. You cannot hear anyone's voice, but consultations and reports develop and dissolve, incessantly. It feels like church.

From the orderlies to the surgeons, there is one purpose, and that is to save lives or heal the wounded. The very young Black woman who greets every arrival immaculate in jeans and a T-shirt is the triage physician, who is embarrassed by the morally questionable principles that underlie her task: "To provide the greatest care to the greatest good," she explains, "you have to sort through the needs and demands of the patients who arrive by ambulance." Dr. Cherie Hardis is, as she says, "obviously sad." Only forty patients related to the earthquake have come in: to the core of her heart, she wishes there had been a deluge but "the ones who needed a lot of stuff never got to the hospital. They were crushed or killed. They never got here, or anywhere."

And still she waits, erect, and eagerly looking out across the emergency-room parking lot; perhaps, after all, there will be more survivors arriving, more help that she can lend, more work for her head and her hands riveted to the deepest promise implied by medical care.

In the desolate half hour that ensues, no new patients arrive.

A contingent of press sweeps into a parking space and reporters pile out. There are so many journalists, now, that Phyllis Brown convenes a press conference in the otherwise empty emergency waiting room.

Dr. Carter Clements is a very young white man standing in jeans with his plaid shirtsleeves rolled up. He is the assistant chief physician for the emergency department and he reports that the support from the health-care agency and the Board of Supervisors has been extraordinary. Furthermore, so many doctors have volunteered there are almost more doctors than patients available. Of the forty to forty-five arrivals since 5:05 P.M., eight have been judged to have sustained critical trauma aggravations of the "blunt-injury" kind.

He speaks of the loss of power that paralyzed the X-ray facilities and meant that no CAT scans and no angiograms have been possible. He tells us that, yes, in the past, there had been serious earthquake drills but "generally it was assumed that some communications would be intact." For several hours, the hospital had no phones. They have been dealing with the consequences of three-and-a-half-foot steel-reinforced concrete slabs falling on cars, wedging cars inextricably into a tangle of fatal mass and crushed-out life.

Everywhere there is an omnipresent and spectacular willing tenderness. "We are helpless," he is saying. "Helpless." Nothing usual applies.

What was needed at the Cypress Section of the 880 freeway was not ambulances, not doctors, not police, not media personnel, but cranes—gigantic-capacity cranes to lift and free the victims from their sudden, awful burial.

It will be twenty-four hours before heavy cranes and cherry pickers reach the concrete cemetery of 880. For everyone at Highland Hospital the terrible hope had become just this: that anyone still trapped by that collapse lost consciousness at once and died, unconscious. Otherwise, well, it was to be hoped that there was no otherwise. To hope for death is such a failure for those who would be merciful, and pain marks all the faces of the waiting staff at Highland Hospital.

In the morning light the TV screen persists in its depiction of the devastation of San Francisco: it is the loss of property against the loss of human life in Oakland. It is the cataclysmic disruption of one city against the finality of death in another.

Earthquake damage is estimated at more than $2 billion. People go begging for water and for food and for blankets. Some fifty miles to the south, the residents of Santa Cruz and Los Gatos belatedly receive media attention. There has been vast tragedy and terror. No one can predict recovery time or cost. For an unknown number of human beings, recovery has become irrelevant: they have been killed by the earthquake of 1989.

And the long-neglected animal settles into uneasy sleep, exhausted by the passion of its outrage. And I am waiting for the unidentified young Black woman, victim of unpardonable violence, to claim her outrage, claim our love.

No
Chocolates
for
Breakfast

VALENTINE'S DAY, 1989. ACTUALLY, ANY VALENTINE'S DAY OF any year is something of a sore point for Black women in white America. Flowers and wine by candlelight have always been pretty scarce items in the housing projects and tenements or raggedy shacks where most of us live, if we have someplace, indoors, to sleep and keep a hard-won semblance of a family alive. They've been scarce, as, oh—let's say—scarce as sweet-talking lovers who stick around, hands-on, to mitigate the Monday-morning blues.

But, meanwhile, we've been managing, you know, entirely without chocolates for breakfast.

For example, I can't think of a single Black woman who has a wife. And I could easily fill the Manhattan Yellow Pages with a list of woeful, specific disadvantages summarized by that fact. And yet we work in greater numbers than our white counterparts. We head more households. By ourselves, we're

This essay was originally published in *The Progressive,* April 1989.

raising the great majority of Black children. We earn less than white men, white women, and Black men, period.

And, none of us has a wife. Not one of us has somebody devoted and programmed to say amazing things like, "That's all right, honey. I'll take care of the laundry—and the garbage," or "Don't worry about it; I'll stay home with Kamali," or "I'll get dinner together," or "I'll clean up," or, most important, "Why don't you just sit down."

But let me not exaggerate the debit side of things! We do have "experts." I bet anybody ten cents: if Black women disappeared tomorrow, a huge retinue of self-appointed and *New York Times*–appointed "experts" would have to hit the streets looking for new jobs.

It seems we can't be beat for blame. I mean, whenever these experts find two or three Black women, why, the next thing you know, there is a pathogenic *This* or a pathological *That*. Seems we're generally not doing good enough or else we're doing altogether too good. Either way, me and my sistren, we apparently function as the hopeless carriers, if not the causative agents, of bad news.

Anyway, Valentine's Day, 1989, and I begin by calling an extremely successful Black woman writer who is the sole support of two sons and who happens to be somebody I love. We do not talk long even though neither of us has to excuse herself and run to the door where Western Union's staggering under a load of passionate telegrams addressed to the one-and-only dearest-treasure-in-the-world, meaning me, or my friend. Immediately afterwards I go into the local stationers and I choose the prettiest, the most delicate and obviously handmade birthday card to send to my friend, whose name day's coming up fast. As I wait to pay the (white) man my $2.50, I spot a Decorative Magnet ("fine porcelain enamel") featuring an absolutely leprous Aunt Jemima. I can feel this homicidal rush of blood to my face. But I'm cool.

"How much," I ask the (white) man behind the counter, "how much is that particular little obscenity over there?"

He eyes me carefully. "Four dollars," he says, but then deciding, I guess, that I'm real keen to remove this lurid affront from the public realm, he tells me, "Five."

Silently, we assess each other. I'm serious. But so is he. I throw five dollars on top of the birthday card and slam back into the street.

No telegram is one thing, but Aunt Jemima on *my* Valentine's Day?

That's about as gratuitous, as malevolent, and as bedeviling as the *New York Times*. Two Sundays ago, front page, they laid out this pseudo-scientific headline with all their usual pomp: EXPERTS FORESEE A SOCIAL GAP BETWEEN SEXES AMONG BLACKS. According to the information the experts selected for evaluation, 60 percent of Black students in colleges and universities are women: i.e., fewer Black men currently attend institutions of higher learning than do Black women. "This imbalance among blacks," the experts proceed to explain, "will have broad, harmful consequences not only on campuses but throughout American society." What a crock of patriarchal malarkey.

Is it God-given that men of whatever description "should" know more, earn more, wield more power than women? I have never heard anybody say that the virtual monopoly of Black men in the realm of public elected office, up to and including the U.S. Congress—this "imbalance," this de facto minority state of affairs for Black women—implies "broad, harmful consequences" to anything. Have you? I have never heard anybody bemoan the fact that Jesse Jackson is not female. Have you?

And besides, there's a whole lot of catching up that's got to happen. I know of a prestigious West Coast university feverishly trying to hire not one but three Black women on its faculty, all at once: imbalanced? Black men constitute 1.9 percent of that total faculty while Black women amount to a pitiful 0.3 percent.

I'll tell you about "harmful": harmful is the manipulation of 0.3 percent and 1.9 percent so that, instead of uniting to demand a more than ludicrous degree of representation *as a people,* we descend into internecine gender wars at our collective expense.

The point is not about Black boys versus Black girls. The point is that, as of 1988, 49 percent of black children, six years old or younger, "live" below the poverty line.

Can anyone doubt that this is a calamity? This will have "broad, harmful consequences not only on campuses, but throughout American society." That Black women are falling behind somewhat more slowly in a single arena of our national life is not disastrous. There is a disaster, yes, and I have every reason to hope that whoever can turn it around will get started very soon, on the straightaway, lucidly antiracist track that will take us, as a people where we need to go.

In the meantime, looking ahead to Valentine's Day, 1990: Can't you guys violate your own traditions and, just once, just for one teeny-weeny year, Can't you tighten your belts, so to speak, and leave us the hell alone? Or, to paraphrase an Aretha Franklin classic: Don't Send Me No Experts; I Need a Man Named Dr. Feelgood—and I could also use me a wife.

Waiting

for

a Taxi

We weren't doing anything. We hadn't hurt anybody, and we didn't want to. We were on holiday. We had studied maps of the city and taken hundreds of photographs. We had walked ourselves dizzy and stared at the other visitors and stammered out our barely Berlitz versions of a beautiful language. We had marveled at the convenient frequency of the Metro and devoured vegetarian crêpes from a sidewalk concession. Among ourselves, we extolled the seductive intelligence and sensual style of this Paris, this magical place to celebrate the two hundredth anniversary of the French Revolution, this obvious place to sit back with a good glass of wine and think about a world lit by longings for *Liberté, Egalité, Fraternité.*

It was raining. It was dark. It was late. We hurried along, punch-drunk with happiness and fatigue. Behind us, the Cathedral of the Sacred Heart glowed ivory and gorgeous in a flattering wash of artificial, mellow light.

This essay was adapted from "Beyond Gender, Race, and Class," a speech delivered by the author at the Eighth Annual Gender Studies Symposium, "Visions and Voices for Change," at Lewis and Clark College, Portland, Oregon, in April 1989. It was published in *The Progressive,* June 1989.

These last hours of our last full day in Paris seemed to roll and slide into pleasure and surprise. I was happy. I was thinking that, as a matter of fact, the more things change, the more things change.

I was thinking that if we, all of us Black, all of us women, all of us deriving from connected varieties of peasant/immigrant/persecuted histories of struggle and significant triumph, if we could find and trust each other enough to travel together into a land where none of us belonged, nothing on earth was impossible anymore.

But then we tried to get a cab to stop for us, and we failed. We tried again, and then again. One driver actually stopped and then, suddenly, he sped away almost taking with him the arm of one of my companions who had been about to open the door to his taxi.

This was a miserable conclusion to a day of so much tourist privilege and delight, a day of feeling powerful because to be a sightseer is to be completely welcome among strangers. And that's the trick of it: No one will say "no" to freely given admiration and respect. But now we had asked for something in return—a taxi. And with that single, ordinary request, the problems of our identity, our problems of power, reappeared and trashed our holiday confidence and joy.

I am looking for a way to catch a taxi. I am looking for an umbrella big enough to overcome the tactical and moral limitations of "identity politics"—politics based on gender, class, or race. I am searching for the language of a new political consciousness of identity.

Many of us function on the basis of habits of thought that automatically concede paramount importance to race or class. These habits may, for example, correlate race with class in monolithic, absolute ways: i.e., white people have, Black people have not, or, poor people equals Black people. Although understandable, these dominating habits of thought tend to deny the full functions of race and class, both.

If we defer mainly to race, then what about realities of class that point to huge numbers of poor white people or severe differences of many kinds among various, sometimes conflicting classes of Black people?

Or, if we attend primarily to factors of class, then we may mislead ourselves significantly by ignoring privileges inherent to white identity, per se, or the socially contemptible status of minority-group members regardless of class.

Both forms of analysis encourage exaggerated—or plainly mistaken—suppositions about racial or class grounds for political solidarity. Equally important, any exclusive mode of analysis will overlook, or obviate, the genuine potential for political unity across class and race boundaries.

Habits of racial and class analyses also deny universal functions of gender which determine at least as much, if not more, about any citizen's psychological, economic, and physical life-force and well-being. Focusing on racial *or* class *or* gender attributes will yield only distorted and deeply inadequate images of ourselves.

Traditional calls to "unity" on the basis of only one of these factors—race or class or gender—will fail, finally, and again and again, I believe, because no single one of these components provides for a valid fathoming of the complete individual.

And yet, many of us persist in our race/class habits of thought. And why is that? We know the negative, the evil origins, the evil circumstances that have demanded our development of race and class analyses. For those of us born into a historically scorned and jeopardized status, our bodily survival testifies to the defensively positive meanings of race and class identity because we have created these positive implications as a source of self-defense.

We have wrested, we have invented positive consequences from facts of unequal conflict, facts of oppression. Facts such as I am Black, or I do not have much money, or I am Lithuanian, or I am Senegalese, or I am a girl, or my father mends shoes, become necessary and crucial facts of race and class and gender inside the negative contexts of unequal conflict and the oppression of one group by another, the oppression of somebody weak by somebody more powerful.

Race and *class*, then, are not the same kinds of words as *grass* and *stars*. *Gender* is not the same kind of noun as *sunlight*. *Grass, stars,* and *sunlight* all enjoy self-evident, positive connotations, everywhere on the planet. They are physical phenomena unencumbered by our knowledge or our experience of slavery, discrimination, rape, and murder. They do not presuppose an evil any one of us must seek to extirpate.

I am wondering if those of us who began our lives in difficult conditions defined by our race or our class or our gender identities, I am wondering if we can become more carefully aware of the limitations of race and class and gender analyses, for these yield only distorted and deeply inadequate images of ourselves.

There is another realm of possibility, political unity and human community based upon concepts that underlie or supersede relatively immutable factors of race, class, and gender: the concept of justice, the concept of equality, the concept of tenderness.

I rejoice to see that, last year, more than eight million American voters—Black and white and Latino and Asian and Native American and straight and gay and lesbian and working-class and Ivy League—voted for Jesse Jackson.

I rejoice to see that 300,000 people demonstrated for pro-choice rights in Washington, D.C., on April 9, 1989. Of that 300,000, an estimated 100,000 who stood up for women's rights were men.

I rejoice at this good news, this happy evidence of moral and tactical outreach and response beyond identity politics. This is getting us where all of us need to go.

On the other hand, the hideous despoiling of Prince William Sound in Alaska, the Exxon spill of ten million gallons of oil contaminating 3,000 square miles of those previously clear and lovely waters, makes plain the total irrelevance—the dismal inadequacy—of identity politics, or even national politics. From the torn sky of Antarctica to the Port of Valdez in Alaska, we need vigilant, international agencies empowered to assure the survival of our life-supporting environments.

But we are creatures of habit. I consider myself fortunate, therefore, to keep coming upon immediate, personal events that challenge my inclinations toward a politics as preoccupied with the known old enemies as it is alert to the potential for new allies.

Less than a month ago, I traveled to Liverpool, England, for the first time. I brought with me a selection of my poetry that includes poems written during the 1960s, during the Civil Rights Revolution. I had heard about the poverty characteristic of much of Liverpool, but I was not ready for what I encountered face to face.

One of my hosts was Ruth Grosvenor, a young Black woman who described herself, at lunch, as a half-caste Irish-Caribbean. I asked her for more detail about her family background, and she told me about her mother, who had grown up in Ireland so poor she regularly used to dig in the pig bins, searching for scraps of edible garbage. And for additional pennies, her mother was given soiled sanitary napkins to launder by hand.

Ruth's mother, of course, is white. I had lost my appetite, by now, completely, and I could not comprehend the evident cheeriness of Ruth, who had moved on in conversation to describe the building success of the Africa Art Collective in Liverpool that she codirects.

"But," I interrupted, "what about your mother? What has happened to her?"

"Oh," Ruth told me, instantly switching subjects but not altering her bright and proselytizing tone, "my mother is very happy. She remarried, and she has her own little flat, at last. And she has a telephone!"

I felt mortified by the contrast between what would allow me, a Black woman from America, to feel happy and the late and minimal amenities that could ease the daily experience of a white woman living in England. To speak with Ruth's mother, to speak for Ruth's mother, I would certainly have to eschew facile notions of race and class correlation. On the basis of class alone, Ruth's mother might very well distrust or resent me. On the basis of race alone, I might very well be inclined to distrust or resent Ruth's mother.

And yet, identity politics aside, we both had infinitely more to gain as possible comrades joined against socioeconomic inequities than we could conceivably benefit from hostilities exchanged in serious ignorance of each other.

After our lunch, we drove to the Liverpool public library, where I was scheduled to read. By then, we were forty-five minutes late, and on arrival we saw five middle-aged white women heading away towards an old car across the street. When they recognized me, the women came over and apologized: They were really sorry, they said, but they had to leave or they'd get in trouble on the job. I looked at them. Every one of them was wearing an inexpensive, faded housedress and, over that, a cheap and shapeless cardigan sweater. I felt honored by their open-mindedness in having wanted to come and listen to my poetry. I thought and I said that it was I who should apologize: I was late. It was I who felt, moreover, unprepared: what in my work, to date, deserves the open-minded attention of blue-collar white women terrified by the prospect of overstaying a union-guaranteed hour for lunch?

Two and a half weeks after Liverpool, I sat sorting through my messages and mail at the university where I teach. One message kept recurring: A young Black man—the son, in fact, of a colleague—had been accused of raping a young white woman. The message, as delivered by my secretary, was this: Call So-and-So at once about the young Black man who supposedly raped some white woman.

I was appalled by the accusation leveled against the son of my colleague. I was stunned to learn that yet another female student, of whatever color, had been raped. I felt a kind of nausea overtaking me as I reread the phone messages. They seemed to assume I would commit myself to one side or the other, automatically. The sides, apparently, were Young Black Man versus Young White Woman.

I got up from my desk and snatched the nearest newspaper I could find. I needed to know more. As best I could tell, the young Black student could not have raped anybody; he had several witnesses who established him off campus throughout the evening of the alleged assault. As far as I can tell, the young white woman had been raped and she was certain, if mistaken, about the face and the voice of her assailant.

I declined to make any public comment: I do not yet know what the truth of this terrible matter may be. I believe there is a likelihood of mistaken identification on the part of the victim. And I believe that such a mistake, if that is the case, will have created a second victim, the wrongly accused Black student. But these are my opinions merely. And I cannot comprehend why or how anyone would expect me to choose between my gender and racial identities.

I do not agree that rape is less serious than any other heinous felony. I do not agree that the skin color of a female victim shall alienate me from a gender sense of unity and peril. I do not agree that the mistaken accusation of a Black man is less than a very serious crime. I do not agree that the genuine gender concerns that I embody shall alienate me from a racial sense of unity and peril.

But there is a route out of the paralysis of identity politics, even here, in this ugly, heartbreaking crisis. There is available to me a moral attachment to a concept beyond gender and race. I am referring to the concept of justice, which I am prepared to embrace and monitor so that justice shall equally serve the young Black man and the young white woman. It is that concept and it is on behalf of both the primary and the possible second victim of yet another on-campus rape that I am willing to commit my energies and my trust.

Returning to the recent rainy evening in Paris, I am still looking for an umbrella big enough to overcome the tactical and moral limitations of identity politics.

Yes, I am exhilarated by the holiday I enjoyed with my friends, and I am proud of the intimate camaraderie we shared. But somebody, pretty soon, needs to be talking, sisterly and brotherly, with the taxi drivers of the world, as well.

THE

DANCE

OF

REVOLUTION

As a favor to me
Let's not talk any more about old dances.
I have an entire world on the tip of my tongue.

—*Cornelius Eady,* from "Victims of the Latest Dance Craze"

EVERY ONCE IN A WHILE, IT HAPPENS. YOU CAN'T EVEN PREDICT or block this ugly, overwhelming kind of thing. Suddenly, you're writhing flat at the absolute bottom of your morale. Nothing important or good seems possible. And the enemies strike. And the enemies strike again.

Perhaps they will kill the waters of Prince William Sound. You cannot visualize this horror but you can feel the hideous choke, the gagging agony, ten million gallons of oil spilling into one helpless throat of the earth. And what is to be done?

Or, yet another woman falls victim to male violence. Is it a white woman jogging in the park? Is it a Black woman, as she approaches the building where she lives? Is it a Latino woman

This essay was originally published in *The Progressive,* August 1989.

who finds obscene and threatening notes stuffed under the windshield wipers of her car? Was one of these women well-educated or working-class or well-to-do or ambitious or friendly or pregnant or Republican or busy or tired or the newlywed wife of the man who beat her to death?

Like the pristine waters of Alaska, the human female of the species cannot escape an apparently American continuum of gratuitous and savage hostility or neglect. Whether it's a multi-national corporation destroying irrecoverable and lovely parts of our world or suburban teenagers choosing to gang-rape and sodomize a high school classmate ("Anyway, she was sort of retarded, so what's the big deal?"), the ruinous legacy of violence neither shrinks nor fades in the light of another day. And you know it, you accept that you may formulate political protest or privately comfort a friend, but you can neither cure nor overcome the consequences of defilement and contempt.

Everything appears familiar and doomed. Nothing looks clear or tractable or positively guaranteed. And so, even if you come upon a city reservoir standing full and sweet and open to the skies above Baltimore, for example, your unavoidable second thoughts will emanate from automatic fears for its safety, and your own. The commonplace face of your mother/your sister/your daughters/your wife/your girlfriend will trigger concern: what are their day-by-day chances up against an omnipresent, statistical countdown to terror and attack beyond recovery?

And so you capitulate to all the bad news: you retreat. "What is to be done?" slurs into "What difference does it make?" Horror and rage capsize into bitterness and self-pity, and the screaming of your soul confirms the wisdom of a miserable inertia. Reaching backwards, you embrace perspectives quite inimical to hope. As Keats wrote, these times lead you to the valleys of the spirit "where but to think is to be full of sorrow / And leaden-eyed despairs."

And, because there is no such thing as a politics of futility, questions of courage or cowardice do not arise. Issues of right and wrong fail to bestir any response. You push along, slowly, from one terrible loss to the next. For sure, you cannot save anything or anybody from the destruction that now preoccupies your mind. Evil is old. Evil is long and powerful and everywhere. You unplug the telephone and call it a night.

Repeatedly, this happens. And so you stick it out. You put your money on surprise, and you wait.

Two months ago, I was waiting for a really big surprise. I needed one. And, sure enough, the world, entirely outside my control, astounded and aroused my sleeping heart.

First, I happened upon a poem by the young Black poet, Cornelius Eady, whose lines appear at the beginning of this column. Cornelius was not born to silver spoons or crystal stairs. Cornelius is not stupid or unconscious. But his poetry just flies along with generosity, wit, sexy good sense, and joy. And I thought, "If Cornelius can hang in here, happily, then who am I to moan and groan around the house?"

Second, some friends of mine were visiting from England and, because I knew they were "over the moon" fans of Madonna, I checked the papers to see what might be happening. On May 24, 1989, at the Brooklyn Academy of Music, we found a benefit concert, "Don't Bungle the Jungle!," hosted by Madonna and Kenny Scharf. Starring the B52's. Rob Wasserman and Bob Weir, and the Del Fuegos, among others, the concert raised money and consciousness for the rain forest in Brazil.

My friends and I attended this event. Impatiently we sat through various performances, waiting for Madonna. At the conclusion of the concert, comedian-singer Sandra Bernhard walked on stage looking gorgeous and wrapped in an American flag while she carried lit incense pushed into the end of an extremely bizarre cigarette holder. After delivering an alternately hilarious and impassioned jeremiad that rallied the crowd against AIDS/homophobia/homelessness/racism and official indifference, she invited the audience to welcome "somebody."

Madonna appeared, dressed in an outfit identical to Bernhard's and, following a final recitation of facts about the jungle (every second an area of tropical forest the size of a football field is lost forever), launched into a fabulous jump-rendition of the venerable Sonny and Cher classic, "I've Got You Babe." Well, to the complete amazement of everyone present, Madonna and Sandra Bernhard then clasped hands and, in each other's arms, sang Sonny Bono's song again, this time as a duet:

. . . I got you to hold my hand
I got you to understand
I got you to kiss goodnight
I got you to hold me tight.

As the London *Daily Sun* reported, May 26, 1989, front page: "The Love Birds . . . stunned an audience with their lesbian romp." As a matter of fact, I never before in my whole life saw anything like it. I could hardly breathe. And when they finished the song, I was on my feet, along with the rest of that packed Brooklyn throng, cheering for them. Talk about guts! Talk about news! Talk about exhilaration of the soul!

Eleven days later, I stared at that lone Chinese man who stood in front of the advancing line of tanks at Tiananmen Square in Beijing. Inside the tank, another man had to stop or run over—and crush—his courageous compatriot. The man inside the tank drove to the right, trying to avoid his challenger. The man in the street moved to the right. The tank swerved to the left. The man in the street moved to the left.

They were dancing. The tank resumed its front-and-center position. The man in the street jumped on the tank, and threw his body on top of it. Talk about guts! Talk about news! Talk about exhilaration of the soul! In one week, I had seen the dance and the love that genuine revolution delivers into the world. The courage and the passion of Madonna and Sandra Bernhard in Brooklyn, and then the lone Chinese challenger of Tank Number One on Tiananmen Square have snatched me out of the failings of my own faith.

I am back on the block, looking for trouble and expecting good news, with nothing less than "an entire world on the tip of my tongue."

WHERE
IS
THE RAGE?

EVEN AMONG PEOPLE WHO STILL USE THE "L WORD" TO DE-
scribe themselves, trashing the 1960s as some kind of huge,
juvenile mistake has become quite commonplace. Or we encounter the perversities of history denied (e.g., *Mississippi
Burning*) or we flinch from the well-meant but certainly jejune
manipulation of "Martin," "Malcolm," and Birmingham, Alabama, 1963, in the brave new world according to Spike Lee
(e.g., *Do the Right Thing*).

But maybe that's okay. Superficiality, distortion, and denial
constitute neither wonderful nor heinous events per se. But
nowhere, so far, in this commercial retrospective on a decade
as radical and as consequential as that great American afterthought, the Bill of Rights, nowhere can we find properly
respectful efforts to identify the distinctive mass attributes that
led to a revolution in civil rights at home and a callback of the
troops from abroad.

I think it's about that time.

I think none of us—hindsight wizards that we are—none of us

This essay was originally published in *The Progressive*, October 1989.

has proven ourselves nearly as wise, as effective, as persevering as the myriad and mostly anonymous Americans who fought to desegregate the privileges of freedom and who stopped a war.

Since "The Sixties," what have we accomplished, exactly? If we had anything going for us, anything remotely commensurate to the depth and the force of those now almost unimaginable ten years, we, consequently, would also have universal health care, or a federal megahousing program, or children in totally nonabusive child-care situations, or all of the above, at the least. We need these conditions of being alive every bit as much as we need not to be shot through the head by a sheriff determined to block Black voter registration.

But we possess none of these necessities. And, instead, basic supports for our rightful autonomy as individual citizens, basic guarantees, and bitterly contested entitlements have been taken away from us.

The United States Supreme Court, once a reliable if ultimate recourse for progressive and even revolutionary grievances, has become a retrograde wellspring for enormous economic and social distress. At the end of its 1989 deliberations, the Court could point to no fewer than seven successful attacks against affirmative-action policies and guidelines. That's a lot of damage. Three of the worst rulings are these:

• *Ward's Cove v. Antonio,* which pretty much immunizes the concept of "business necessity" from fair-play scrutiny and assessment.

• *Warren v. AT&T Technologies,* which protects the principle of "seniority" from antidiscrimination challenges to undue work-force homogeneity.

• And, most remarkably, *Martin v. Wilks,* which allows for "reverse discrimination" suits brought by white men, for instance, who might, otherwise, discover themselves a little bit penalized for laziness or inattention. Such plaintiffs can now make their lamentations any number of years after the allegedly objectionable "affirmative action" has taken place. In other words, no statute of limitations controls such shameless claims to injury.

Taken together, these particular Court findings dispute or disregard the separate and altogether unequal histories of women and minorities. They ridicule the grief that underlies the call for reparations or redress. They constitute a racist and sexist assault upon millions of Americans even as they try to deny the reality and meaning of such social disease. And, blithely, they overturn humane functions of the law as it relates to the weak who cannot procure alternatives to state protection of their interests.

In addition, the conservative five-justice majority has jeopardized reproductive choice earlier secured for women in *Roe v. Wade.* And they have extended the death penalty, and they have further curtailed the legal prerogatives of prisoners.

Given the coming consequences of these decisions, public response has been mild. Purporting to reflect our general response, the media have characterized these brutal decrees as "tragic." But "affirmative action" is not an academic subject for comfortable debate. Reproductive choice is not some trendy item to toss or keep around the house. If you cannot get an education or a job, if you cannot choose what will or will not happen with your own body, then what freedom do you have?

I remember the 1960s as first and last enflamed by mass demands for freedom. And I know that the extraordinary tumult of that time produced more freedom in our daily and collective lives than ever imagined by most of us standing shoulder to shoulder and holding hands and singing those songs that seem embarrassing today.

The Sixties worked because we knew that the absence of civil rights did not amount to "tragic" circumstances. Depriving me of my freedom or murdering Vietnamese families in my name was neither unkind nor ineluctable. It was wrong. We used a different language back then. We stood, immovable, because we believed we were right. An upfront moral formulation of the issues did not hurl us into quandaries of rhetoric: the American Left was right, and the rest of America was wrong.

Today, it is the American Right that stands, immovable, because Jesse Helms really believes in the moral rectitude of his perspectives and his vision. He does not equivocate. He does not mourn the loss of any battle; he and his kinsmen become enraged. They beat up Black students, they burn abortion clinics, they hound television stations, art galleries, and legislators in a fearsome fervor. And they get what they want, more and more frequently.

I can remember the rage that convulsed my body and my mind and my imagination when I learned about the racist bombing of the Sixteenth Street Baptist Church in Birmingham and the murder of those Black children. I do not recall any equivocal emotion in my heart. I was livid. That was evil. That was wrong. And, along with a decisive number of other Americans, I was ready for whatever it took to exorcise the hideous power of that hideous hatred from my life.

The neglected legacy of the Sixties is just this: unabashed moral certitude, and the purity—the incredibly outgoing energy—of righteous rage.

I do not believe that we can restore and expand the freedoms that our lives require unless and until we embrace the justice of our rage. And, if we do not change the language of current political discourse, if we do not reintroduce a Right and Wrong, a Good or Evil measurement of doers and deeds, then how shall we, finally, argue our cause?

Now that the Supreme Court has removed itself from humane and democratic functions of the law, shall we persist in beggarly petitions to that agency? Should we surrender our grievances and wither away in civil silence? Have we lost heart? Have the streets and the highways and the bridges of America closed down? Can we not take to them in anger and in expectation of relief? Is it better to scream or to die?

If we are afraid to insist we are right, then what?

On War and War and War and ...

On a recent, cold Sunday morning in Kennebunkport, Maine, George Bush and his wife, Barbara, apparently seated themselves inside a small country church of God. (To think about what?)

Alma Powell, wife of the Joint Chief Commander of U.S. Armed Forces, reports that she likes to keep "comforting foods," like vegetable soup, ready on top of the stove for Colin, her certainly hardworking husband. Alma adds that, these days, she just "knows" that her Colin doesn't want to hear "little stories" about the children.

(Just the soup, ma'am.)

Secretary of Defense Dick Cheney, second only to his boss in bloodthirst for arm's-length/armchair warfare, has never served half an hour, even, in the army, the navy, the air force, or the marines.

(I know; it's not right to pick on him just for that.)

Last Saturday, at a local antiwar rally organized by the Middle East Children's Alliance, I noted, aloud, that the war, to date, was costing us fifty-six billion dollars. Every twenty-four hours, the cost is one billion, at least. I, therefore, proposed the following to the crowd scattered on the grass and under the trees:

One billion dollars a day for seven days for Oakland!
Can you imagine that?
One billion dollars a day!
But to hell with imagination!
This is our city!
This is our money!
These are our lives!
One billion dollars a day for seven days for Oakland!
(Or) do we accept that there is only "the will and the wallet"
when it's about kill or be killed?
Do we need this money or not?
Do we need it here?
Do we need it now? (And so on.)

When I left the stage a reporter came up to me: "You meant one *million* dollars, didn't you?"

"No!" I answered him, amazed: "One billion: one billion dollars a day for seven days for Oakland! That's the bill, that's our bill for housing and drug rehabilitation and books in the public schools and hospital care and all of that good stuff. One billion dollars a day! It's a modest proposal. In less than three months, those maniacs in the White House and the Pentagon have spent fifty-six billion dollars in my name and with my taxes, trying to obliterate Iraq and its people and their leader. I'm saying, call home the troops and the bucks! We need these big bucks to make this a homeland, not a desert, right here, for the troops and for you and for me. What's the problem? It's a bargain! Seven billion dollars on the serious improvement of American life in Oakland versus fifty-six billion dollars for death and destruction inside Iraq! What's the problem?"

But the reporter was giving me a weak smile of farewell that let me understand he found my proposal preposterous. One *million* dollars for life, okay. Billions for kill or be killed, okay. But really big bucks on us, the people of these United States? One billion dollars a day to promote, for example, the safety and educational attainment and communal happiness of 339,000 Americans? I must be kidding!

As I walked away from the park, I felt a heavy depression overtaking me; the reporter, a tall white man with clear eyes, could not contemplate the transfer of his and my aggregate resources from death to life as a reasonable idea. Worse, he could not suppose his and my life to be worth anything close to the value of organized, high-tech, and boastful murder.

But then, other people stopped me to ask, "How can we do that? Do we write letters or what?" And so, as I write this column tonight, I am reassured because not everybody American has lost her mind or his soul. Not every one of my compatriots has become a flag-wrapped lunatic lusting after oil/power/the perversions of "kicking ass," preferably via TV.

A huge number of Americans has joined with enormous numbers of Arab peoples and European communities in Germany, England, France, Italy, Spain, and Muslim communities throughout India and Pakistan to cry out, "Stop!"

And when I say "huge," I mean it: If 1,000 Americans contacted by some pollster can be said to represent 250 million people, then how many multi-multi-millions do we, antiwar movement gatherings of more than 100,000, coast to coast and on every continent, how many do we represent?!

And how come nobody ever does that kind of political math?

And tonight, February 2, 1991, when, yet again, the ruling white men of America despise peace and sneer at negotiations and intensify their arm's-length/armchair prosecution of this evil war, this display of a racist value system that will never allow for any nationalism that is not their own and that will never allow Third World countries to control their own natural resources and that will never ever express, let alone feel, regret or remorse or shame or horror at the loss of any human life that is not white, tonight I am particularly proud to be an African-American.

By launching the heaviest air assault in history against Iraq on January 15, George Bush dared to desecrate the birthday of Martin Luther King, Jr. Tonight (and 83,000 bombing missions later) is the twenty-sixth anniversary of the assassination of Malcolm X. On this sorry evening the world has seen the pathological real deal behind the sanctimonious rhetoric of Bush and Company: The Persian Gulf War is not about Iraqi withdrawal from Kuwait. The war is not about Kuwait at all. Clearly it's not about international law or respect of United Nations' resolutions since, by comparison to Washington, Tel Aviv, and Pretoria, "the Butcher of Baghdad" is a minor league Johnny-Come-Lately to the realm of outlaw conduct and contempt for world opinion!

What has happened tonight is that the Soviet leader, Mikhail Gorbachev, and the government of Iraq have reached an agreement whereby Iraq would withdraw from Kuwait and that is a fact—regardless of anything else included or omitted by the proposal. This agreement should provide for immediate cease-fire, a cessation of the slaughter of Iraqi men and women and a halt to the demolition, nationwide, of their water supply, their access to food, their securement of shelter.

So what is the response of the Number One White Man in America? He's gone off "to the theater." I guess that means that the nearest church was closed. Or that Colin Powell was busy dipping his spoon into the comfort of a pot of soup somebody else cooked for him. And that Dick Cheney was fit to be tied into any kind of uniform so long as it meant nobody would take away his Patriot missiles and Apache helicopters and B-52 cluster-bomb bombers and Black and Brown and poor White soldiers and sailors and all the rest of these toys for a truly big-time coward.

Confronted with the "nightmare" prospect of peace, Bush

goes off to the theater because he'll be damned if he will acknowledge that Saddam Hussein is a man, is the head of a sovereign state, is an enemy to be reckoned with, an opponent with whom one must negotiate: Saddam Hussein is not a white man! He and his Arab peoples must be destroyed! No peace! No cease-fire! No negotiations!

And I am proud tonight to remember Dr. King and Malcolm X, and to mourn their absence, even as I pursue the difficult challenge of their legacy. Both of these men became the targets of white wrath when they, in their different ways, developed into global visionaries persisting against racism in Alabama, in Harlem, in South Africa, in Vietnam. Neither of these men could have failed to condemn this current attack against the Arab world. Neither of these men ever condoned anything less than equal justice and equal rights. Hence, the undeniably racist double standards now levied against Saddam Hussein would have appalled and alienated both of them, completely.

I am proud to shake hands with the increasing number of African-American conscientious objectors. I am proud to re-mark the steadfast moral certainty of U.S. Congressman Ronald Dellume's opposition to this war. I am proud to hear about the conscientious objections of congressmen Gus Savage and John Conyers and Mervyn Dymally. I am proud to observe that, even while African-Americans remain disproportionately repre-sented in the U.S. armed forces, we, as a national community, stand distinct, despite and apart from all vagaries of popular opinion; we maintain a proportionately higher-than-white level of opposition to this horrible war, this horrendous evasion of domestic degeneration and decay.

And I want to say something else, specific to you, Mr. Presi-dent: It's true you can humiliate and you can hound and you can smash and burn and terrify and smirk and boast and defame and demonize and dismiss and incinerate and starve and, yes, you can force somebody, force a people, to surrender what remains of their bloody bowels into your grasping, bony, dry hands.

But all of us who are weak, we watch you. And we learn from your hatred. And we do not forget.

And we are many, Mr. President. We are most of the people on this godforsaken planet.

A New Politics of Sexuality

As a young worried mother, I remember turning to Dr. Benjamin Spock's *Common Sense Book of Baby and Child Care* just about as often as I'd pick up the telephone. He was God. I was ignorant but striving to be good: a good Mother. And so it was there, in that best-seller pocketbook of do's and don't's, that I came upon this doozie of a guideline: Do not wear miniskirts or other provocative clothing because that will upset your child, especially if your child happens to be a boy. If you give your offspring "cause" to think of you as a sexual being, he will, at the least, become disturbed; you will derail the equilibrium of his notions about your possible identity and meaning in the world.

It had never occurred to me that anyone, especially my son, might look upon me as an asexual being. I had never supposed that "asexual" was some kind of positive designation I should, so to speak, lust after. I was pretty surprised by Dr. Spock. However, I was also, by habit, a creature of obedience. For a

This essay was adapted from the author's keynote address to the Bisexual, Gay, and Lesbian Student Association at Stanford University on April 29, 1991. It was published in *The Progressive,* July 1991.

couple of weeks I actually experimented with lusterless colors and dowdy tops and bottoms, self-consciously hoping thereby to prove myself as a lusterless and dowdy and, therefore, excellent female parent.

Years would have to pass before I could recognize the familiar, by then, absurdity of a man setting himself up as the expert on a subject that presupposed women as the primary objects for his patriarchal discourse—on motherhood, no less! Years passed before I came to perceive the perversity of dominant power assumed by men, and the perversity of self-determining power ceded to men by women.

A lot of years went by before I understood the dynamics of what anyone could summarize as the Politics of Sexuality.

I believe the Politics of Sexuality is the most ancient and probably the most profound arena for human conflict. Increasingly, it seems clear to me that deeper and more pervasive than any other oppression, than any other bitterly contested human domain, is the oppression of sexuality, the exploitation of the human domain of sexuality for power.

When I say sexuality, I mean gender: I mean male subjugation of human beings because they are female. When I say sexuality, I mean heterosexual institutionalization of rights and privileges denied to homosexual men and women. When I say sexuality I mean gay or lesbian contempt for bisexual modes of human relationship.

The Politics of Sexuality therefore subsumes all of the different ways in which some of us seek to dictate to others of us what we should do, what we should desire, what we should dream about, and how we should behave ourselves, generally. From China to Iran, from Nigeria to Czechoslovakia, from Chile to California, the politics of sexuality—enforced by traditions of state-sanctioned violence plus religion and the law— reduces to male domination of women, heterosexist tyranny, and, among those of us who are in any case deemed despicable or deviant by the powerful, we find intolerance for those who choose a different, a more complicated—for example, an interracial or bisexual—mode of rebellion and freedom.

We must move out from the shadows of our collective subjugation—as people of color/as women/as gay/as lesbian/as bisexual human beings.

I can voice my ideas without hesitation or fear because I am speaking, finally, about myself. I am Black and I am female and I am a mother and I am bisexual and I am a nationalist and I am an antinationalist. And I mean to be fully and freely all that I am!

Conversely, I do not accept that any white or Black or Chinese man—I do not accept that, for instance, Dr. Spock—should presume to tell me, or any other woman, how to mother a child. He has no right. He is not a mother. My child is not his child. And, likewise, I do not accept that anyone—any woman or any man who is not inextricably part of the subject he or she dares to address—should attempt to tell any of us, the objects of her or his presumptuous discourse, what we should do or what we should not do.

Recently, I have come upon gratuitous and appalling pseudoliberal pronouncements on sexuality. Too often, these utterances fall out of the mouths of men and women who first disclaim any sentiment remotely related to homophobia, but who then proceed to issue outrageous opinions like the following:

• That it is blasphemous to compare the oppression of gay, lesbian, or bisexual people to the oppression, say, of black people, or of the Palestinians.
• That the bottom line about gay or lesbian or bisexual identity is that you can conceal it whenever necessary and, so, therefore, why don't you do just that? Why don't you keep your deviant sexuality in the closet and let the rest of

us—we who suffer oppression for reasons of our ineradicable and always visible components of our personhood such as race or gender—get on with our more necessary, our more beleaguered struggle to survive?

Well, number one: I believe I have worked as hard as I could, and then harder than that, on behalf of equality and justice—for African-Americans, for the Palestinian people, and for people of color everywhere.

And no, I do not believe it is blasphemous to compare oppressions of sexuality to oppressions of race and ethnicity: Freedom is indivisible or it is nothing at all besides sloganeering and temporary, short-sighted, and short-lived advancement for a few. Freedom is indivisible, and either we are working for freedom or you are working for the sake of your self-interests and I am working for mine.

If you can finally go to the bathroom wherever you find one, if you can finally order a cup of coffee and drink it wherever coffee is available, but you cannot follow your heart—you cannot respect the response of your own honest body in the world—then how much of what kind of freedom does any one of us possess?

Or, conversely, if your heart and your honest body can be controlled by the state, or controlled by community taboo, are you not then, and in that case, no more than a slave ruled by outside force?

What tyranny could exceed a tyranny that dictates to the human heart, and that attempts to dictate the public career of an honest human body?

Freedom is indivisible; the Politics of Sexuality is not some optional "special-interest" concern for serious, progressive folk.

And, on another level, let me assure you: if every single gay or lesbian or bisexual man or woman active on the Left of

American politics decided to stay home, there would be *no* Left left.

One of the things I want to propose is that we act on that reality: that we insistently demand reciprocal respect and concern from those who cheerfully depend upon our brains and our energies for their, and our, effective impact on the political landscape.

Last spring, at Berkeley, some students asked me to speak at a rally against racism. And I did. There were four or five hundred people massed on Sproul Plaza, standing together against that evil. And, on the next day, on that same plaza, there was a rally for bisexual and gay and lesbian rights, and students asked me to speak at that rally. And I did. There were fewer than seventy-five people stranded, pitiful, on that public space. And I said then what I say today: That was disgraceful! There should have been just one rally. One rally: freedom is indivisible.

As for the second, nefarious pronouncement on sexuality that now enjoys mass-media currency: the idiot notion of keeping yourself in the closet—that is very much the same thing as the suggestion that black folks and Asian-Americans and Mexican-Americans should assimilate and become as "white" as possible—in our walk/talk/music/food/values—or else. Or else? Or else we should, deservedly, perish.

Sure enough, we have plenty of exposure to white everything so why would we opt to remain our African/Asian/Mexican selves? The answer is that suicide is absolute, and if you think you will survive by hiding who you really are, you are sadly misled: there is no such thing as partial or intermittent suicide. You can only survive if you—who you really are—do survive.

Likewise, we who are not men and we who are not heterosexist—we, sure enough, have plenty of exposure to male-dominated/heterosexist this and that.

But a struggle to survive cannot lead to suicide: suicide is the opposite of survival. And so we must not conceal/assimilate/integrate into the would-be dominant culture and political system that despises us. Our survival requires that we alter our environment so that we can live and so that we can hold each other's hands and so that we can kiss each other on the streets, and in the daylight of our existence, without terror and without violent and sometimes fatal reactions from the busybodies of America.

Finally, I need to speak on bisexuality. I do believe that the analogy is interracial or multiracial identity. I do believe that the analogy for bisexuality is a multicultural, multi-ethnic, multiracial world view. Bisexuality follows from such a perspective and leads to it, as well.

Just as there are many men and women in the United States whose parents have given them more than one racial, more than one ethnic identity and cultural heritage to honor; and just as these men and women must deny no given part of themselves except at the risk of self-deception and the insanities that must issue from that; and just as these men and women embody the principle of equality among races and ethnic communities; and just as these men and women falter and anguish and choose and then falter again and then anguish and then choose yet again how they will honor the irreducible complexity of their God-given human being—even so, there are many men and women, especially young men and women, who seek to embrace the complexity of their total, always-changing social and political circumstance.

They seek to embrace our increasing global complexity on the basis of the heart and on the basis of an honest human body. Not according to ideology. Not according to group pressure. Not according to anybody's concept of "correct."

This is a New Politics of Sexuality. And even as I despair of identity politics—because identity is given and principles of justice/equality/freedom cut across given gender and given racial definitions of being, and because I will call you my brother, I will call you my sister, on the basis of what you *do* for justice, what you *do* for equality, what you *do* for freedom and *not* on the basis of who you are, even so I look with admiration and respect upon the new, bisexual politics of sexuality.

This emerging movement politicizes the so-called middle ground: Bisexuality invalidates either/or formulation, either/or analysis. Bisexuality means I am free and I am as likely to want and to love a woman as I am likely to want and to love a man, and what about that? Isn't that what freedom implies?

If you are free, you are not predictable and you are not controllable. To my mind, that is the keenly positive, politicizing significance of bisexual affirmation:

To insist upon complexity, to insist upon the validity of all of the components of social/sexual complexity, to insist upon the equal validity of all of the components of social/sexual complexity.

This seems to me a unifying, 1990s mandate for revolutionary Americans planning to make it into the twenty-first century on the basis of the heart, on the basis of an honest human body, consecrated to every struggle for justice, every struggle for equality, every struggle for freedom.

Toward

a Manifest

New

Destiny

Three of the four Noble Truths articulated by
Buddha, upon his enlightenment, in his first sermon:

The First Noble Truth is that all
beings are subject to suffering. No one
escapes . . . suffering is universal.
The Second Noble Truth is that the
cause of suffering is ignorance. And
ignorance of oneself is the greatest
ignorance.
The Third Noble Truth is that
ignorance, the cause of suffering, can be
overcome.

—c. 428 B.C.

"Manifest Destiny":

—First used in the U.S. Congress on January 3, 1846, by Representative
Robert C. Winthrop of Massachusetts, who spoke on the subject of "the
right of our manifest destiny to spread over this whole continent."

This essay was adapted from a speech delivered at Mount Holyoke College on
December 8, 1991. It was published in *The Progressive*, February 1992. The author
wishes to thank Ron Takaki and Margaret Lin for their invaluable guidance in
research for this essay.

THIRTY YEARS AGO, WHITE PUBLICATIONS LOVED TO HEADLINE stories about my neighborhood, my family, and me, with three words: "The Negro Problem."

I remember rapid adjustment of my mind from a state of plain puzzlement to anger. I'd be passing by a subway newsstand and there I'd see it, that incendiary formulation that implied that we, "Negroes," had created our own difficulties and, further, that we, "Negroes," were the only ones who could, or should, give a damn. So many Americans succumbed to that game!

Again and again, slick magazines and daily papers blamed the victim and erased, or exculpated, the perpetrators of the crime. This was all the more remarkable as the context was one of wild white violence, which meant that Negro "difficulties" might well include catching a bullet in the brain if your local sheriff discovered you trying to register to vote.

What finally blew away these print-media fabrications—what finally replaced them with factual knowledge leading to a national and worldwide uproar that, in turn, led to the Civil Rights Act of 1960 and other pivotal laws—was the camera: Regardless of the caption beneath the photograph, regardless of the text read by the (white) voice-over on film, visual reports of our history carried the day. You could not watch a white man screaming as he overturned, set afire, and burned up a Greyhound bus and then still be confused about who, exactly, had done what, where, and when.

I wonder what it will take to blow away an equally fictitious, an equally venomous print-media construction of our time: the so-called Politically Correct or PC Controversy.

I would like to assume that an eyeball basis for analysis and opinion could decide things. And perhaps, at the last, that will happen. But I cannot forget going on a lunch date, once, with Victor Navasky, editor of *The Nation*.

We met at his office above the congestion of Fourteenth

Street in Manhattan. As we walked to the restaurant of his choice, a few blocks away, we moved among and around crowds of Black and Puerto Rican as well as white New Yorkers. I was asking Victor how come *The Nation* had never hired a single Black columnist. He seemed exasperated by my inquiry. He could not comprehend how anything calling itself *The Nation* but staffed entirely by white men could seem peculiar, if not offensive, to anyone. He could not imagine that an American who was different from himself in serious, immutable ways—he could not imagine that such an American writer might bring to *The Nation* something important: information and perspectives that he and his white associates could not otherwise encounter or possess.

"Are you saying," he asked in an avuncular tone, "are you implying that there is A Black Point of View?"

I answered him—"Yes"—and I attempted to explain that there is an absolute difference between his white male history and my own. I argued that such a chasmic separation in experience must produce significant divergences of viewpoint, expectations, and the like.

But Victor was not interested. Comfortably seated at his regular table inside his restaurant of choice, he knew something I was only beginning to understand: There is difference, and there is power. And who holds the power shall decide the meaning of difference. Victor held the power, and he had decided that ideas and opinions and feelings that belong to anybody markedly different from himself are ideas and convictions that do not count.

Victor embodies a one-man definition—a big part, the American media part—of the problem of knowledge in the United States. Too much of what we know or don't know depends upon unaccountable individual values and the sometimes whimsical happenstance of one man's or one powerful family's or one corporate CEO's political biography. In the case of Navasky, here was a white man blind and deaf except to a mirror universe of his kin and kind. And what could I do about it?

I have worked here, inside this country, and I have kept my eyes open, everlastingly. What I see today does not support a media-concocted controversy where my life or the lives of African-Americans, Native Americans, Chicano-Americans, Latin-Americans, and Asian-Americans amount to arguable fringe or freak components of some theoretical netherland. We have become the many peoples of this nation—nothing less than that. I do not accept that we, American peoples of color, signify anything optional or dubious or marginal or exotic or anything in any way less valuable, less necessary, less sacred than white America.

I do not perceive current issues of public education as issues of politically correct or incorrect curriculum. In a straight line back to James Baldwin who, twenty-eight years ago, begged us, Blackfolks, to rescue ourselves by wrestling white people out of the madness of their megalomania and delusion. I see every root argument about public education turning upon definitions of sanity and insanity. Shall we submit to ceaseless lies, fantastic misinformation, and fantastic omissions? Shall we agree to the erasure of our beleaguered, heterogeneous truth? Shall we embrace traditions of insanity and lose ourselves and the whole real world?

Or shall we become "politically correct" as fast as we can and defend and engage the multifoliate, overwhelming, and ultimately inescapable actual life that our myriad and disparate histories imply?

In America, in a democracy, who shall the people know if not our many selves? What shall we aim to learn about the universe if not the entire, complicated truth of it, to the best of our always limited abilities? What does public education in a democratic state require if not the rational enlightenment of as many of the people as possible? But how can you claim to enlighten a child and then tell him that the language of his mother is illegal?

BARCO DE REFUGIADOS

Mamá me crío sin lenguaje.
Soy huérfano de mi nombre español.
Las palabras son extrañas,
tartamudeando en mi lengua.
Mis ojos ven el espejo, mi reflejo:
piel de bronce, cabello negro.

Siento que soy un cautivo
a bordo de un barco de refugiados.
El barco que nunca atraca.
El barco que nunca atraca.

REFUGEE SHIP

Mama raised me without language.
I'm orphaned from my Spanish name.
The words are foreign, stumbling
on my tongue. I see in the mirror
my reflection: bronzed skin, black
  hair.

I feel I am a captive
aboard the refugee ship.
The ship that will never dock.
El barco que nunca atraca.
                    —Lorna Dee Cervantes[1]

White warriors for the preservation of the past and for a mythical status quo, white warriors for the insane, invoke supposedly scary scenarios in which Platonic dialogues disappear from the core of academic studies and students instead examine the teachings of Buddha or the political writings of

---

[1]This poem is reprinted by permission of Lorna Dee Cervantes.

Frederick Douglass. I look at these mainly conjectural outbursts and I say to myself, "What's all the fuss about?"

The favorite, last-resort accusation of these white warriors for the insane, for the traditional white-male-dominated canon of required readings in American higher education, is this: that the barbarian leadership of us, the barbarian hordes, basically aims to subvert and challenge and eliminate the intellectual icons of Western civilization. Commonly, this accusation produces a good deal of apologetic shuffling on the part of the alleged barbarians, the so-called Politically Correct. Well, I am one barbarian who will not apologize. You bet that's one of my basic aims! Why would anyone suppose that I or any Native American or any Asian-American would willingly worship at the altar of traditional white Western iconography?

As the contradiction among the features
creates the harmony of the face
we proclaim the oneness of the suffering
and the revolt
of all the peoples on all the face of the earth
and we mix the mortar of the age of brotherhood
out of the dust of idols.
   —Jacques Roumain, "Bois-d'Ebène"

The gods of the white Western world, from Jahweh ("Vengeance is mine, saith the Lord") to Jesus ("Blessed are the meek") to Dante to Nietzsche to Milton to T. S. Eliot to Wallace Stevens: What have they done for me? Show me one life saved by any of these gods! Show me one colored life!

As you descend deeper and deeper into media hysteria about alleged or impending "violations of the canon" and "rape of the foundations of Western civilization," the smell of brain rot and unmitigated white supremacist ideology becomes unmistakable.

Suppose, for example, suppose I skipped English literature and Shakespeare altogether and instead I studied Chinese: Chinese history and Chinese literature. A quarter of the human beings on the planet are Chinese. And I know next to nothing about them. I do not really understand why my friend who was born in the Year of the Dragon cannot marry her beloved who was born in the Year of the Dog. But I can recite to you a score of beautiful lines from Elizabethan sonnets. And I do not altogether fault what I know, but I do not view my ignorance as acceptable. And if I had to choose between those sonnets and Chinese history, and if I chose Chinese history, who could criticize me, and on what grounds?

It depends, of course, on the purpose of education. Uncontested, until now, the purpose of American schooling has been to maintain the powerful in power. And so, traditional materials for the American classroom have presented every war, every battle, every dispute, every icon of knowledge required by "higher" education in the image of the powerful so as to serve the interests of the powerful who need the rest of us to believe they are really nice guys who take off their boots before they take over your house and your land.

Reinforcing the skewed effects of traditional materials is the homogeneous identity of teachers and faculty who persist, increasingly out of sync, with the heterogeneous student bodies whose intellectual development they must oversee. For example, in California public schools, teachers remain 82 percent white while so-called minority students occupy 54 percent of classroom seats. Such a dramatic disjuncture does not bode well for imperative curricular change that will serve the cultural and historical needs of these new (young) Americans.

Supreme Court Justice Clarence Thomas—whose four law clerks are, every one of them, white men, and whose accomplishments as former head of the Equal Employment Opportunity Commission do not cleanly distinguish him from David Duke— wonderfully illustrates the results of traditional "higher" American education. So do those Japanese-Americans who cannot proclaim, too fervently or too frequently, how lamentable was the Japanese bombing of Pearl Harbor.

If you're not white, if you're not an American white man, and you travel through the traditional twistings and distortions of the white Western canon, you stand an excellent chance of ending up *nuts:* estranged if not opposed to yourself and your heritage and, furthermore, probably unaware of your estrangement, your well-educated self-hatred.

The last seven days leading to the fiftieth anniversary of Pearl Harbor were particularly difficult. At moments, I felt overwhelmed as the coast-to-coast unanimity of know-nothing, racist blatherings about December 7, 1941, grew louder and ever more obviously self-righteous and unbalanced by even a respectable modicum of trustworthy scholarship or unbiased inquiry into the Japanese side of the story.

Of course, any concern to secure the Japanese side of the story would represent a concern that is Politically Correct. It would mean supposing that the Japanese people are not some subspecies of the human race, alias *Homo americo,* or whatever. It would mean supposing that the Japanese government did not lapse into a psychotic military fit that fateful morning but that, in fact, the Japanese government had its reasons for attacking that rather far-flung U.S. naval base, Pearl Harbor.

And I have been nauseated by the unmitigated, ignorant, hate-mongering sanctimony of American leaders these past seven days. Is there, after all, another country as militaristic, as predatory, as imperial, as deadly as our own? Does the average American even have the glimmer of an adequate, sane education to respond to that question?

The lunacy of racist America, the insanity of Politically Incorrect education in racist America, means that it's okay to advertise the atomic bombing of Hiroshima as "revenge" for the Japanese bombing of Pearl Harbor.

Asian peoples are the largest group of human beings on the planet. This kind of pathological, complacent Asian-bashing is truly not all right: not morally or intellectually or, in any wise, defensible, sane behavior. And when I must wallow in this latest display of America's latest racist target—a target jeopardizing most of the human beings on the planet—then, yes, I get pretty damned upset. Here is a quote from the front page of *USA Today*, December 6, 1991:

> By 1941, Japan's campaign of Asian conquest was ten years old. Over Western protests the Japanese war machine had occupied Manchuria and invaded China. After the occupation of French Indochina, the United States, Britain, and the Netherlands imposed a trade embargo, cutting Japan's oil supplies by 90 per cent. Japan quickly turned its attention to expropriating oil fields in the Dutch East Indies. To prevent U.S. interference, Tokyo mounted a bold plan to wipe out the U.S. fleet at Pearl Harbor, Hawaii, on December 7, 1941.

Okay. "By 1941, Japan's campaign of Asian conquest was ten years old." By 1941, how old was America's and England's and the Netherlands' campaign of Asian conquest? And what in the hell are you talking about when you say "French Indochina" and the "Dutch East Indies"?

Here is a poem that no English major in the U.S.A. will ever be required to read: it was written by the Japanese-Canadian poet and novelist Joy Kogawa, and it's entitled "Hiroshima Exit."

In round round rooms of our wanderings
Victims and victimizers in circular flight
Fact pursuing fact
Warning leaflets still drip down

On soil heavy with flames.
Black rain, footsteps, witnessings—

The Atomic Bomb Memorial Building:
A curiosity shop filled with
Remnants of clothing, radiation sickness.
Fleshless faces, tourists muttering
"Well, they started it."
Words jingle down
"They didn't think about us
in Pearl Harbor."
They? Us?
I tiptoe around the curiosity shop
Seeking my target
Precision becomes essential
Quick. Quick. Before he's out of range.
Spell the name
America?
Hiroshima?

Air raid warnings wail bleakly
Hiroshima
Morning.
I step outside
And close softly the door
Believing, believing
That outside this store
Is another door

The annual American commemoration of Pearl Harbor of-
fers as hateful a case history of racist miseducation according
to the canon as any. Is there any other occasion on which the
United States catapults into national acrobatics about having
been caught off guard, caught by an enemy first strike?

If December 7, 1941, is "A Day of Infamy," what should we
call August 6, 1945?

Why is the Japanese attack on Pearl Harbor so particularly
galling and humiliating as to merit racist designation as a
"Black Day" in American history?

Why do we remember Pearl Harbor and not V-J Day? Why do we forget February 19, 1942, *that* Day of Infamy, when Franklin Roosevelt signed Executive Order 9066, whereby 100,000 innocent Japanese and Japanese-Americans were sentenced to American concentration camps? What is the difference between A Sneak Attack or A Terrorist Attack and, on the other hand, A Surprise Attack, A Brilliant Military Maneuver, A Pre-emptive Strike, or A Massive Allied Air Assault?

Is there a difference between the U.S. military base of Pearl Harbor and the Japanese civilian city of Hiroshima?

Is there any difference between a wartime buddy of George Bush—a buddy flying a naval attack plane on a wartime mission against Japan—and 130,000 Japanese men, women, and children, civilians living in the civilian city of Hiroshima, where they were mass-murdered, mass burned to death or deformed into a living death within five minutes of the United States dropping the "Unthinkable Weapon," the atom bomb? Is there any difference?

What was the difference between official U.S. treatment accorded to German-Americans, Italian-Americans, and Japanese-Americans during World War II?

What's the difference between a German, an Italian, and somebody Japanese? Why were Germans and German-Americans and Italians and Italian-Americans *not* rounded up and sent to American concentration camps in World War II? Why were only those Japanese-Americans living on the West Coast sent to concentration camps?

Did you ever learn/did your teachers ever tell you that a higher percentage of Americans of Japanese ancestry ended up serving in the U.S. Army during World War II *than any other racial group*?

Did you know that until 1943 federal law prohibited foreign-born Chinese from becoming American citizens?

Did you know that until 1952 federal law prohibited foreign-born Japanese from becoming Americans?

Did you know that, having already segregated Chinese and Korean children, the San Francisco School Board in 1907 voted to segregate the total of the *100* Japanese children living there?

Is it possible that the Japanese government copped an attitude, at any point, toward the racist American policies and laws imposed upon Japanese people trying to live and work hard in the United States?

Question: Why am I always talking about racism, anyway?

Did you know that the Naturalization Act of 1790 decreed that only white people could become naturalized citizens of the United States?

Did you know that the Naturalization Act of 1790 fused all peoples of color into the damned and the despised and the legally unprotected American "underclass" now clamoring to overthrow The Canon that doesn't ever mention Hiroshima while it most certainly requires you to read Matthew Arnold, the nineteenth-century poet, essayist, and arrogant jerk who pretty much invented White Poetry—or the notion of touchstones of Great Poetry—all of the touchstones being, as it happens, white male poets: Dante, Goethe, Pound, Eliot, Stevens, Heaney.

Because most well-educated Americans would have to answer, "I don't know" or "I didn't know" in response to that foregoing batch of test questions, a virulent Oreo phenomenon like Clarence Thomas becomes a probability rather than a shock.

And, on another level, Japan-bashing/Asian-bashing continues to flourish and intensify, even among other despised American groups who should know better.

How can anybody get past the ignorance that the American media and the academic canon guarantee?

It's not easy. A friend of mine, the preeminent scholar of Asian-American history, Ron Takaki, was recently told by Howard Goldberg of the *New York Times* that the *New York Times* was feeling "frankly over-Japanned." Moreover, Goldberg summarily dismissed Takaki as "dead wrong" because Takaki had dared to disagree with Goldberg about Pearl Harbor. Takaki had argued that there is both American and Japanese responsibility for that attack, and for the commencement of the Pacific war. Accordingly, Goldberg characterized Takaki's op-ed piece as "revisionist history" and, therefore, decided not to allow Takaki to appear on the *New York Times* op-ed page.

It's not easy. But most Americans are not even distant relatives of the nice guys who run the country. And so there's not a lot of emotional blur to our perceptions. We've had to see them as clearly as the hunted need to watch the ones who hunt them down. Even without the overdue and radical reform of American education that sanity and democracy demand, some of us have learned more than we ever wanted to know about those nice guys.

Some of us sit in front of a young man, a member of the Creek nation, and we hear his voice break and we feel his hands trembling and we avoid staring at the tears that pour from his eyes as he tells us about the annihilation of his ancestors, about the bashing of babies' heads against trees, and about the alternate, nearly extinct world view that his forefathers and foremothers embraced. Between convulsions of grief, he speaks about the loss of earlier, spirit relations between his hungering people and the foods of the earth.

Some of us must devise and improvise a million and one ways to convince young African-American and Chicana women that white skin and yellow hair and blue eyes and thin thighs are not imperative attributes of beauty and loveliness.

Some of us must reassure a student born and raised in Hong Kong that we do not ask her to speak aloud in order to ridicule her "English" but in order to benefit from the wisdom of her intelligence.

Some of us search for avenues or for the invention of avenues for African-American boys to become men among men beyond and without surrendering to that racist offering of a kill-or-be-killed destiny.

And we move among the peoples of this nation on an eyeball basis. We do not deny the heterogeneity that surrounds our bodies and our minds. We do not suppress the variegated sounds of multiple languages spoken by so many truly different Americans all in one place, hoping for love.

Over the last three semesters, I've been teaching a series of experimental poetry classes at the University of California, Berkeley. As of last spring, the enthusiastic, diverse, campus-wide student response led me to offer what I call Poetry for the People. Centered on student writings, this course publishes student poetry and presents these new poets in public readings of their work.

The ethnic, racial, intellectual, and sexual diversity of these students has forced me to attempt to devise a syllabus that is, for me, unprecedented, and even unwieldy, in its range. And for the first time I've had to ask for help from a diverse number of student teacher poets as well as other faculty, in order to handle the course materials responsibly.

The idea behind Poetry for the People is that every man or woman can be enabled to use language with the precision and the memorable impact that poetry requires. In this way, the writing and publishing and public presentation of poetry becomes a process of empowerment for students as well as a catalyst for coalition politics of a practical and spontaneous nature.

Student readings have been attended by standing-room-only crowds, without exception. Required books for the course include Native American, Chicana/Chicano, white poetry,

African-American poetry, women's poetry, Asian-American poetry.

And so I am trying to become Politically Correct. I am just one among an expanding hard-core number of American educators who believe that an American culture requirement, for instance, is not a laughable or subversive or anti-intellectual proposal: on the contrary! We are teachers running as fast as we can to catch up with the new Americans we are paid to educate.

In 1987, the Hudson Institute released a report entitled "Workfare 2000." According to the *San Francisco Chronicle,* "the report stunned American business leaders with its projection that in the remaining years of this century, *only 15 per cent of the entrants into the workforce would be white males.*" (My italics.)

That's nationwide.

By the year 2010, California's population will nearly double, and this will be the racial breakdown: overall, 61 percent people of color; 39 percent non-Hispanic white; 38 percent Hispanic; 16 percent Asian; 7 percent black.

From that total population, we will have to publicly educate nearly twice as many students as the total number in 1991. What will we teach these new Americans? How will we seek to justify every lecture, every homework assignment?

In 1992—right now—this is the composition of the freshman class at UC-Berkeley, reputedly the best public university in the United States: 30 percent white; 31.5 percent Asian; 20.5 percent Hispanic; 7.5 percent Black; i.e., 59.5 percent people of color.

And so, walking across this American campus, you will see, as I have seen, on an eyeball basis, that this America of ours is changing faster than fast—although the faculty at Berkeley remains 89 percent white, which represents only a 2 percent decrease of white faculty members during the last ten years.

The current distribution and identity of power will have to change, as well, or we will have to laugh the word *democracy* out of our consciousness forever.

And that is the political crisis that each of us personifies, one way or the other.

Since the demographics of our nation state do not even forecast English as the usual first language of most of our future children, what is the meaning of "English only" legislation, for example, in the state of California?

What does that reveal besides the politics of culture?

And who shall decide what these many peoples of America shall know or not know?

And what does that question underscore besides the political nature of knowledge?

And what shall be the international identity and what shall be the national identity of these United States when a white majority no longer exists inside our boundaries even as a white majority has never existed beyond these blood-and-gore-begotten boundaries of our nation-state?

I do not agree that I am a statistical component of some alarming controversy. The indisputable value of each and every one of our lives is not debatable, is *not* politically correct or incorrect.

In this crisis of American power, in this conflict between power and human life, *there can be no canon, there can be no single text for the education of our multicultural, multilingual, multiracial population!*

Some thirty years ago, in his "Letter to My Nephew," James Baldwin wrote the following:

> Know whence you came. If you know whence you came, there is really no limit to where you can go. The details and symbols of our life have been deliberately constructed to make you believe what white people say

about you. Please try to remember that what they believe, as well as what they do and cause you to endure, does not testify to your inferiority but to their inferiority and fear.

And, in that same letter, he wrote:

If the word *integration* means anything, this is what it means: That we, with love, shall force our brothers to see themselves as they are, to cease fleeing from reality and begin to change it.

And so I propose that we undertake to make of the teachings of public education in America a politically correct, a verifiably sane basis for our multicultural, multiracial, and two-gendered lives on this infinitely multifaceted, multilingual planet. I propose that we undertake this awesome work with pride and, yes, fanatical zeal.

It seems to me that this Year of the Ram, this moment of ours, is just an obvious, excellent moment to declare for America, and for ourselves, a Manifest New Destiny: a destiny that will extricate all of us from the sickness of egomania and ignorance, a destiny that will cherish and delight in the differences among us, a destiny that will depend upon empowerment of the many and merciful protection of the young and the weak, a destiny that will carry us beyond an eyeball basis of knowledge into an educated, collective vision of a really democratic, a really humane, a really really good time together.

Can I
Get
a Witness?

I WANTED TO WRITE A LETTER TO ANITA HILL. I WANTED TO SAY thanks. I wanted to convey the sorrow and the bitterness I feel on her behalf. I wanted to explode the history that twisted itself around the innocence of her fate. I wanted to assail the brutal ironies, the cruel consistencies that left her—at the moment of her utmost vulnerability and public power—isolated, betrayed, abused, and not nearly as powerful as those who sought and who seek to besmirch, ridicule, and condemn the truth of her important and perishable human being. I wanted to reassure her of her rights, her sanity, and the African beauty of her earnest commitment to do right and to be a good woman: a good black woman in this America.

But tonight I am still too furious, I am still too hurt, I am still too astounded and nauseated by the enemies of Anita Hill. Tonight my heart pounds with shame.

Is there no way to interdict and terminate the traditional, abusive loneliness of black women in this savage country?

From those slavery times when African men could not dare

This essay was originally published in *The Progressive,* December 12, 1991.

to defend their sisters, their mothers, their sweethearts, their wives, and their daughters—except at the risk of their lives—from those times until today: Has nothing changed?

How is it possible that only John Carr—a young black corporate lawyer who maintained a friendship with Anita Hill ten years ago ("It didn't go but so far," he testified, with an engaging, handsome trace of a smile)—how is it possible that he, alone among black men, stood tall and strong and righteous as a witness for her defense?

What about spokesmen for the NAACP or the National Urban League?

What about spokesmen for the U.S. Congressional Black Caucus?

All of the organizational and elected black men who spoke aloud against a wrong black man, Clarence Thomas, for the sake of principles resting upon decency and concerns for fair play, equal protection, and affirmative action—where did they go when, suddenly, a good black woman arose among us, trying to tell the truth?

Where did they go? And why?

Is it conceivable that a young white woman could be tricked into appearing before twelve black men of the U.S. Senate?

Is it conceivable that a young white woman could be tricked into appearing before a lineup of incredibly powerful and hypocritical and sneering and hellbent black men freely insinuating and freely hypothesizing whatever lurid scenario came into their heads?

Is it conceivable that such a young woman—such a flower of white womanhood—would, by herself, have to withstand the calumny and unabashed, unlawful bullying that was heaped upon Anita Hill?

Is it conceivable that this flower would not be swiftly surrounded by white knights rallying—with ropes, or guns, or whatever—to defend her honor and the honor, the legal and civilized rights, of white people, per se?

Anita Hill was tricked. She was set up. She had been minding her business at the University of Oklahoma Law School when the senators asked her to describe her relationship with Clarence Thomas. Anita Hill's dutiful answers disclosed that Thomas had violated the trust of his office as head of the Equal Employment Opportunity Commission. Sitting in that office of ultimate recourse for women suffering from sexual harassment, Thomas himself harassed Anita Hill, repeatedly, with unwanted sexual advances and remarks.

Although Anita Hill had not volunteered this information and only supplied it in response to direct, specific inquiries from the FBI.

And although Anita Hill was promised the protection of confidentiality as regards her sworn statement of allegations.

And despite the fact that four witnesses—two men and two women, two black and two white distinguished Americans, including a federal judge and a professor of law—testified, under oath, that Anita Hill had told each of them about these sordid carryings on by Thomas at the time of their occurrence or in the years that followed,

And despite the fact that Anita Hill sustained a remarkably fastidious display of exact recall and never alleged, for example, that Thomas actually touched her,

And despite the unpardonable decision by the U.S. Senate Judiciary Committee to prohibit expert testimony on sexual harassment,

Anita Hill, a young black woman born and raised within a black farm family of thirteen children, a graduate of an Oklahoma public high school who later earned honors and graduated from Yale Law School, a political conservative and, now, a professor of law,

Anita Hill, a young black woman who suffered sexual harassment once in ten years and, therefore, never reported sexual harassment to any of her friends except for that once in ten years,

Anita Hill, whose public calm and dispassionate sincerity refreshed America's eyes and ears with her persuasive example of what somebody looks like and sounds like when she's simply trying to tell the truth,

Anita Hill was subpoenaed by the U.S. Senate Judiciary Committee of fourteen white men and made to testify and to tolerate interrogation on national television.

1. Why didn't she "do something" when Thomas allegedly harassed her?

The senators didn't seem to notice or to care that Thomas occupied the office of last recourse for victims of sexual harassment. And had the committee allowed any expert on the subject to testify, we would have learned that it is absolutely typical for victims to keep silent.

2. Wasn't it the case that she had/has fantasies and is delusional?

Remarkably, not a single psychiatrist or licensed psychologist was allowed to testify. These slanderous suppositions about the psychic functionings of Anita Hill were never more than malevolent speculations invited by one or another of the fourteen white senators as they sat above an assortment of character witnesses handpicked by White House staffers eager to protect the president's nominee.

One loathsomely memorable item: John Doggett, a self-infatuated black attorney and a friend of Clarence Thomas, declared that Thomas would not have jeopardized his career for Anita Hill because Doggett, a black man, explained to the Senate Committee of fourteen white men, "She is not worth it."

3. Why was she "lying"?

It should be noted that Anita Hill readily agreed to a lie-detector test and that, according to the test, she was telling the truth. It should also be noted that Clarence Thomas refused even to consider taking such a test and that, furthermore, he had already established himself as a liar when, earlier in the Senate hearings, he insisted that he had never discussed *Roe v. Wade,* and didn't know much about this paramount legal dispute.

Meanwhile, Clarence Thomas—who has nodded and grinned his way to glory and power by denying systemic American realities of racism, on the one hand, and by publicly castigating and lying about his own sister, a poor black woman, on the other—this Thomas, this Uncle Tom calamity of mediocre abilities, at best, this bootstrap miracle of egomaniacal myth and self-pity, this choice of the very same president who has vetoed two civil-rights bills and boasted about that, how did he respond to the testimony of Anita Hill?

Clarence Thomas thundered and he shook. Clarence Thomas glowered and he growled. "God is my judge!" he cried, at one especially disgusting low point in the Senate proceedings. "God is my judge, Senator. And not you!" This candidate for the Supreme Court evidently believes himself exempt from the judgments of mere men.

This Clarence Thomas—about whom an African-American young man in my freshman composition class exclaimed, "He's an Uncle Tom. He's a hypocritical Uncle Tom. And I don't care what happens to his punk ass"—this Thomas vilified the hearings as a "high-tech lynching."

When he got into hot water for the first time (on public record, at any rate), he attempted to identify himself as a regular black man. What a peculiar reaction to the charge of sexual harassment!

And where was the laughter that should have embarrassed him out of that chamber?

And where were the tears?

When and where was there ever a black man lynched because he was bothering a black woman?

When and where was there ever a white man jailed or tarred and feathered because he was bothering a black woman?

When a black woman is raped or beaten or mutilated by a black man or a white man, what happens?

To be a black woman in this savage country: is that to be nothing and no one beautiful and precious and exquisitely compelling?

To be a black woman in this savage country: is that to be nothing and no one revered and defended and given our help and our gratitude?

The only powerful man to utter and to level the appropriate word of revulsion as a charge against his peers—the word was "SHAME"—that man was U.S. Senator Ted Kennedy, a white man whose ongoing, successful career illuminates the unequal privileges of male gender, white race, and millionaire-class identity.

But Ted Kennedy was not on trial. He has never been on trial.

Clarence Thomas was supposed to be on trial but he was not: he is more powerful than Anita Hill. And his bedfellows, from Senator Strom Thurmond to President George Bush, persist—way more powerful than Clarence Thomas and Anita Hill combined.

And so, at the last, it was she, Anita Hill, who stood alone, trying to tell the truth in an arena of snakes and hyenas and dinosaurs and power-mad dogs. And with this televised victimization of Anita Hill, the American war of violence against women moved from the streets, moved from hip-hop, moved from multimillion-dollar movies into the highest chambers of the U.S. government.

And what is anybody going to do about it?

I, for one, I am going to write a letter to Anita Hill. I am going to tell her that, thank God, she is a black woman who is somebody and something beautiful and precious and exquisitely compelling.

And I am going to say that if this government will not protect and defend her, and all black women, and all women, period, in this savage country—if this government will not defend us from poverty and violence and contempt—then we will change the government. We have the numbers to deliver on this warning.

And, as for those brothers who disappeared when a black woman rose up to tell the truth, listen: It's getting to be payback time. I have been speaking on behalf of a good black woman. Can you hear me?

Can I get a witness?

Requiem

for

the Champ

Mike Tyson comes from Brooklyn. And so do I. Where he grew up was about a twenty-minute bus ride from my house. I always thought his neighborhood looked like a war zone. It reminded me of Berlin—immediately after World War II. I had never seen Berlin except for black-and-white photos in *Life* magazine, but that was bad enough: Rubble. Barren. Blasted. Everywhere you turned your eyes recoiled from the jagged edges of an office building or a cathedral, shattered, or the tops of apartment houses torn off, and nothing alive even intimated, anywhere. I used to think, "This is what it means to fight and really win or really lose. War means you hurt somebody, or something, until there's nothing soft or sensible left."

For sure I never had a boyfriend who came out of Mike Tyson's territory. Yes, I enjoyed my share of tough guys and/ or gang members who walked and talked and fought and loved in quintessential Brooklyn ways: cool, tough, and deadly serious. But there was a code as rigid and as romantic as anything that ever made the pages of traditional English literature. A

This essay was originally published in *The Progressive*, February 1992.

guy would beat up another guy or, if appropriate, he'd kill him. But a guy talked different to a girl. A guy made other guys clean up their language around "his girl." A guy brought ribbons and candies and earrings and tulips to a girl. He took care of her. He walked her home. And if he got serious about that girl, and even if she was only twelve years old, then she became his "lady." And woe betide any other guy stupid enough to disrespect that particular young black female.

But none of the boys—none of the young men—none of the young Black male inhabitants of my universe and my heart ever came from Mike Tyson's streets or avenues. We didn't live someplace fancy or middle-class, but at least there were ten-cent gardens, front and back, and coin Laundromats, and grocery stores, and soda parlors, and barber shops, and Holy Roller churchfronts, and chicken shacks, and dry cleaners, and bars-and-grills, and a takeout Chinese restaurant, and all of that usable detail that docs not survive a war. That kind of seasonal green turf and daily-life supporting pattern of establishments to meet your needs did not exist inside the gelid urban cemetery where Mike Tyson learned what he thought he needed to know.

I remember when the City of New York decided to construct a senior housing project there, in the childhood world of former heavyweight boxing champion Mike Tyson. I remember wondering, "Where in the hell will those old people have to go in order to find food? And how will they get there?"

I'm talking godforsaken. And much of living in Brooklyn was like that. But then it might rain or it might snow and, for example, I could look at the rain forcing forsythia into bloom or watch how snowflakes can tease bare tree limbs into temporary blossoms of snow dissolving into diadems of sunlight. And what did Mike Tyson ever see besides brick walls and garbage in the gutter and disintegrating concrete steps and boarded-up windows and broken car parts blocking the sidewalk and men, bitter, with their hands in their pockets, and women, bitter, with their heads down and their eyes almost closed?

In his neighborhood, where could you buy ribbons for a girl, or tulips?

Mike Tyson comes from Brooklyn. And so do I. In the big picture of America, I never had much going for me. And he had less. I only learned, last year, that I can stop whatever violence starts with me. I only learned, last year, that love is infinitely more interesting, and more exciting, and more powerful, than really winning or really losing a fight. I only learned, last year, that all war leads to death and that all love leads you away from death. I am more than twice Mike Tyson's age. And I'm not stupid. Or slow. But I'm Black. And I come from Brooklyn. And I grew up fighting. And I grew up and I got out of Brooklyn because I got pretty good at fighting. And winning. Or else, intimidating my would-be adversaries with my fists, my feet, and my mouth. And I never wanted to fight. I never wanted anybody to hit me. And I never wanted to hit anybody. But the bell would ring at the end of another dumb day in school and I'd head out with dread and a nervous sweat because I knew some jackass more or less my age and more or less my height would be waiting for me because she or he had nothing better to do than to wait for me and hope to kick my butt or tear up my books or break my pencils or pull hair out of my head.

This is the meaning of poverty: when you have nothing better to do than to hate somebody who, just exactly like yourself, has nothing better to do than to pick on you instead of trying to figure out how come there's nothing better to do. How come there's no gym/no swimming pool/no dirt track/no soccer field/no ice-skating rink/no bike/no bike path/no tennis courts/no language arts workshop/no computer science center/no band practice/no choir rehearsal/no music lessons/no basketball or baseball team? How come neither one of you has his or her own room in a house where you can hang out and dance and make out or get on the telephone or eat and drink up everything in the kitchen that can move? How come nobody on your block and nobody in your class has any of these things?

I'm Black. Mike Tyson is Black. And neither one of us was ever supposed to win anything more than a fight between the two of us. And if you check out the mass-media material on "us," and if you check out the emergency-room reports on "us," you might well believe we're losing the fight to be more than our enemies have decreed. Our enemies would deprive us of everything except each other: hungry and furious and drug-addicted and rejected and ever convinced we can never be beautiful or right or true or different from the beggarly monsters our enemies envision and insist upon, and how should we then stand, Black man and Black woman, face to face?

Way back when I was born, Richard Wright had just published *Native Son* and, thereby, introduced white America to the monstrous product of its racist hatred.

Poverty does not beautify. Poverty does not teach generosity or allow for sucker attributes of tenderness and restraint. In white America, hatred of Blackfolks has imposed horrible poverty upon us.

And so, back in the thirties, Richard Wright's Native Son, Bigger Thomas, did what he thought he had to do: he hideously murdered a white woman and he viciously murdered his Black girlfriend in what he conceived as self-defense. He did not perceive any options to these psychopathic, horrifying deeds. I do not believe he, Bigger Thomas, had any other choices open to him. Not to him, he who was meant to die like the rat he, Bigger Thomas, cornered and smashed to death in his mother's beggarly clean space.

I never thought Bigger Thomas was okay. I never thought he should skate back into my, or anyone's community. But I did and I do think he is my brother. The choices available to us dehumanize. And any single one of us, Black in this white country, we may be defeated, we may become dehumanized, by the monstrous hatred arrayed against us and our needy dreams.

And so I write this requiem for Mike Tyson: international celebrity, millionaire, former heavyweight boxing champion of the world, a big-time winner, a big-time loser, an African-American male in his twenties, and, now, a convicted rapist.

Do I believe he is guilty of rape?

Yes I do.

And what would I propose as appropriate punishment?

Whatever will force him to fear the justice of exact retribution, and whatever will force him, for the rest of his damned life, to regret and to detest the fact that he defiled, he subjugated, and he wounded somebody helpless to his power.

And do I therefore rejoice in the jury's finding?

I do not.

Well, would I like to see Mike Tyson a free man again?

He was never free!

And I do not excuse or condone or forget or minimize or forgive the crime of his violation of the young Black woman he raped!

But did anybody ever tell Mike Tyson that you talk different to a girl? Where would he learn that? Would he learn that from U.S. Senator Ted Kennedy? Or from hotshot/scot-free movie director Roman Polanski? Or from rap recording star Ice Cube? Or from Ronald Reagan and the Grenada escapade? Or from George Bush in Panama? Or from George Bush and Colin Powell in the Persian Gulf? Or from the military hero flyboys who returned from bombing the shit out of civilian cities in

Iraq and then said, laughing and proud, on international TV: "All I need, now, is a woman"? Or from the hundreds of thousands of American football fans? Or from the millions of Americans who would, if they could, pay surrealistic amounts of money just to witness, up close, somebody like Mike Tyson beat the brains out of somebody?

And what could which university teach Mike Tyson about the difference between violence and love? Is there any citadel of higher education in the country that does not pay its football coach at least three times as much as the chancellor and six times as much as its professors and ten times as much as its social and psychological counselors?

In this America where Mike Tyson and I live together and bitterly, bitterly, apart, I say he became what he felt. He felt the stigma of a priori hatred and intentional poverty. He was given the choice of violence or violence: the violence of defeat or the violence of victory. Who would pay him to rehabilitate inner-city housing or to refurbish a bridge? Who would pay him what to study the facts of our collective history? Who would pay him what to plant and nurture the trees of a forest? And who will write and who will play the songs that tell a guy like Mike Tyson how to talk to a girl?

What was America willing to love about Mike Tyson? Or any Black man? Or any man's man?

Tyson's neighborhood and my own have become the same no-win battleground. And he has fallen there. And I do not rejoice. I do not.

PERMISSIONS

ACKNOWLEDGMENTS

Grateful acknowledgment is made to the following for permission to reprint previously published material:

Doubleday: "The Waking" from *The Collected Poems of Theodore Roethke* by Theodore Roethke. Copyright 1953 by Theodore Roethke. Reprinted by permission of Doubleday, a division of Bantam Doubleday Dell Publishing Group, Inc.

The Estate of James Baldwin: Excerpt from "Letter to My Nephew" in *The Fire Next Time* by James Baldwin. Reprinted by permission.

Grove Press Inc.: Excerpt from "Bois-d'Ebène" by Jacques Roumain in *Black Skin, White Masks* by Frantz Fanon. Reprinted by permission.

Joy Kogawa: "Hiroshima Exit" by Joy Kogawa from *Breaking Silence: An Anthology of Contemporary Asian American Poets,* edited by Joseph Bruchac. Reprinted by permission.

Virago Press Ltd.: "The Mountain and the Man Who Was Not God" from *Moving Toward Home: Selected Political Essays* by June Jordan. Copyright © 1981, 1985, 1989 by June Jordan. Published by Virago Press Ltd. in 1989. Reprinted by permission.

Warner/Chappell Music, Inc.: Excerpt from the song lyrics "I Got You Babe" by Sonny Bono. Copyright © 1965 by Cotillion Music, Inc., and Chris Marc Music. All rights administered by Warner-Tamerlane Publishing Corp. All rights reserved. Used by permission.

ABOUT THE AUTHOR

JUNE JORDAN was born in Harlem and raised in the Bedford-Stuyvesant neighborhood of Brooklyn. She studied at the University of Chicago and Barnard College. An essayist and poet, she has written sixteen books, among them *Naming Our Destiny* (poetry); *Moving Towards Home* (essays); *Lyrical Campaigns* (poetry); *On Call* (essays); *Living Room: New Poems, 1980–1984; Civil Wars: Selected Essays, 1963–1980; Things That I Do in the Dark: Selected Poems 1954–1977; Kimako's Story* and *Passion: New Poems 1977–1980*. Her work has also appeared in publications such as *The New York Times, Essence, Esquire, Ms., The Village Voice, The Washington Post, The New Republic, The Nation,* and *The Boston Globe*. Ms. Jordan is the recipient of numerous awards and honors, including a Rockefeller Grant, an NEA Fellowship, and the Prix de Rome. She has taught at the University of Wisconsin, SUNY–Stony Brook, CCNY, Sarah Lawrence College, Yale University, and Connecticut College. She is currently a regular political columnist for *The Progressive* magazine and a professor of Afro-American studies at the University of California at Berkeley.